MEDIT

OF VIRGINIA SATIR

Peace Within, Peace Between, Peace Among

MEDITATIONS OF VIRGINIA SATIR
Peace Within, Peace Between, Peace Among

Edited by

ANNE BANMEN and JOHN BANMEN

Science and Behavior Books, Inc.
Palo Alto, California

Printed in the United States of America.

Library of Congress Card Number 90-062015
ISBN 0-8314-0077-3

Cover design by Lynn Marsh
Manuscript editing by Rain Blockley
Interior design by Gary LaRochelle/Flea Ranch Graphics
Interior art by Barry Ives
Typesetting by BookPrep
Production Editing by Jim Nageotte
Printing by Haddon Craftsmen

Contents

About the Authors

Preface

Virginia Satir usually began her workshops with a meditation to help participants relax and center themselves. Her lovely words of inspiration also stimulated the use of right-brain functions, our base of creativity. During her last visit with us in our home, in March 1988, Virginia shared some thoughts about herself and her use of meditation. The short introduction that follows is her description of the use and meaning she made of her meditations.

We began compiling this book because of our deep love and respect for our friend Virginia and our wish to share her poetic messages with the world. It was an arduous task in the beginning, due to the vast amount of material we considered and sorted through in our wish to include a broad sampling of her meditations.

This book is organized by the sequence in which Virginia developed her meditations. It starts with those that focus on breathing and relaxation, and then moves to meditations about each individual's uniqueness, self-value, and manifestation of life. The emphasis then goes to people's internal resources and energies, followed by looking at having choices, making choices, and sorting our psychological closets. This helps us accept what fits and let go of what no longer fits or is helpful.

Next comes the push toward greater personal integration and further growth toward wholeness and congruence. Finally, the book focuses on what Virginia called the sanctuary, *The Book of Me,* and the self-esteem maintenance kit. These developments in her approach to meditation often include a spiritual aspect of life, which she emphasized more forcefully during her later years.

The poems in this book have an interesting background. Some are by Anne Banmen. Some are from Virginia's material. Others are from specific meditations by Virginia and are presented here in poetic form; these are identified as being by both Virginia and Anne. John Banmen helped with the editing.

During the final years of her life, Virginia traveled around the world with her teachings. She became more and more focused on world peace. As part of her approach toward this goal, she taught that we all need to have peace within before we can have peace between us, and we need peace between people before we can have peace among us. The meditations in this book cover all three aspects so well that we have, at her urging, used the subtitle *Peace Within, Peace Between, Peace Among.*

Following Virginia's death on 10 September 1988, this project took on a new meaning. It is our memorial tribute to Virginia Satir, a spirit pure in essence.

—ANNE BANMEN

JOHN BANMEN

How To Use This Book

We do not intend this book to be read cover to cover in one sitting like a good novel. Each meditation stands on its own and can be read separately. Each deserves its own attention. Allow the full impact of its message to penetrate to your innermost depths.

Any of these meditations can also be read at the opening or closing of a workshop or meeting. When time allows, you can stay longer with the meditation, welcoming the message, contemplating its significance, and practicing its instructions.

You might read these meditations onto cassette tapes and add some meditative background music. You can then listen to them whenever you choose.

A certain amount of repetition exists among these meditations. Virginia Satir found this kind of repetition very comforting, reassuring, settling, and useful. Its effect is similar to what children enjoy when parents repeat favorite bedtime stories night after night. Our attempt here is to balance the centering effect of repetition with plenty of variation in material.

How I Use Meditations
BY VIRGINIA SATIR

People often ask what the purpose is in my use of meditations. I could say it is an overall thing. Everything contained in my teachings has a basis in my meditations, and the reverse is also true; everything in these meditations is basic and connected to my teachings of my "Growth Model." Another way of saying this is that, to me, all these meditations are anchors for growth through the right hemisphere of the brain: anchors for growth within the self.

Meditations have to be positive and are directed through the intuitive, psychic part of ourselves. The way I construct meditations is first to create a pathway to the intuitive part, the sensing part of the self. Then I go to the physical part of the self: for example, the breathing. I connect the breathing with relaxation, which gives one a sense of power and empowerment. People can learn consciously to breathe and relax and enjoy a new sense of strength. For me, breathing and relaxation equals strength. Also, the conscious effort of breathing and relaxing helps pull together various scattered components, again giving a person a sense of power.

With that sense of power, what immediately follows is a positive thought about oneself—loving oneself. Moving from a sense of breathing to relaxation provides an almost automatic result of a positive sense of self.

Through meditations, it is as though I'm doing an internal job of bringing together everything that people have—through their senses, through their feelings about themselves, and through their breathing and relaxation. With this pulling together of various scattered components, people are able to approach the task of tapping their resources.

I know that the ability we have to go into the unknown is due to the resources we have, not because we know what is there or are guaranteed specific outcomes. Knowing about my resources, I can go anywhere, because I take them with me. So if I can center people and allow them to become aware of their resources, that will take them somewhere more hopeful. Then I can reduce their fears about changing.

In my meditations, the centering of the self is a preparation for an integration. My meditations are not just a journey or a visualization, as many others seem to be. What I am working toward in all my meditations is a higher sense of self-worth, a greater trust in the power of the self, and a grounding, anchoring, and expanding of positive uses of our resources.

To the process of using the intuitive hemisphere of the brain, breathing and relaxing, and centering to gain strength, I have added the utilization of internal, personal resources. This helps people go where they have never been before. Therefore, I have added to my meditations:

- The sanctuary, where everything is exactly the way you like it to be

- The self-esteem maintenance kit, with
     a detective hat
     a medallion
     a golden key
     a wishing stick or wand
     a wisdom box

- *The Book of Me,* which is housed in the sanctuary

With these additions, my meditations are not only integrative but also take people into new places and levels of being.

Another aspect of my meditations is letting go, instead of getting rid of that which no longer fits. Reframing what we no longer need and letting it go with a blessing, because it did serve a purpose in the past, makes room in our psychological closet. I find "letting go" is a totally different attitude from "getting rid of."

I am always interested in the fact that people call meditations hypnosis. I see meditations as a path to the intuitive part of ourselves, which I feel is where everything emanates from. Meditating is not an intellectual process, even though we use thought. I never use the word hypnosis. It has too many fears attached to it that suggest a lack of control rather than an enrichment of the power within.

Meditations have to come from a state of love. They have to come from caring, and they have to come from a total belief in growth. The loving and caring also provide a sense of safety. Therefore, before I lead a meditation, I need to prepare myself to be in that state of love and caring. Otherwise meditations are only words, pictures, and instructions. So it is not only what you say but what state you are in. I sit down, relax, and give myself permission to move into my own intuitive state before leading a meditation. Most of the time all I need to do is center myself and I am connected with my inner source of energy, my life force.

My meditations are directional, forward looking. Forwardness is the way growth goes. Therefore I use words, color, sound, metaphors, and a process that moves forward.

Sometimes with people I am new to, without yet a level of trust, I might say, "I would like to start this meeting/workshop with a meditation." Then I talk to them about it. I tell them that the meditation is an opportunity to begin to have that luxurious experience of being totally with oneself. And I might ask, "How many of you have ever had such an experience?" Then I might ask those who have had such an experience to raise their hands. If not many raise a hand, I make a humorous crack and say that we have among us a lot of virgins, and then invite them to try this meditation on for size.

At other times I might introduce meditations by talking about the two hemispheres of our brain: our cognitive and intuitive parts. I explain that outside the intellectual part is the part where all new things initiate, and therefore I will use a meditation to tap that resource, that place.

My overall goal in meditation is to help people to be what I know they can become. The picture I have is that most people's possibilities are sealed off or cut off, and so their behavior manifests itself destructively, or at best in a dull way. I want to reach those parts where the life energy is and let its door open gently. It is like touching something and inviting it to open. My connection with the universe is important, especially during meditation, and I hope to help others with their connection with the universe.

People often tell me my meditations are so powerful. I think what they are telling me is that they had a sense of their own power, a sense of change, of the power of themselves. I immediately take their awareness from me to them and validate their own power and their resources. I never want anything I say to be anything except growth producing.

You can read my meditations out loud, silently to yourself, or out loud to others. You may have them read to you, or read them into a tape recorder and play them back. Some people might make drawings while listening to the meditations. Many people, including me, like appropriate background music with my meditations. Music during meditations connects with all the energies; music is vibration. If you use music that has positive vibrations, it can move you toward greater openness and willingness to move toward a sense of well being and high self-esteem. It is another way to help life find a voice and an expression.

When I start with a meditation, I often ask people to close their eyes. They order their eyes to close, and their eyes close. They don't push, they don't pull, they don't offer their eyes anything, and yet, as a result of a thought, their eyes close. This connection between thought and body response is very important. Whenever you have a thought that is life and death based and you follow any negative expectations, you move toward death. When you follow any positive expectations, you move toward life. What I want to do is to help people understand the connectedness of thought and body response, and its many possibilities in our growth towards congruence and high self-esteem.

Two words have become very important to me in the last two years: hungry and wounded. I can translate anything negative that people do to one another out of hunger and woundedness. Hunger has various levels, all the levels of the mandala: hungry for love, hungry for recognition, hungry for being seen and heard, hungry for stimulation, hungry all over the place. I find the idea of hunger more appropriate than the idea of need. Needs seem more related to physiological aspects such as food, shelter, and clothing. At the basis of these levels of hunger are the yearnings for wholeness, congruence, and connectedness.

The second word shows through the early stages of our growing up. If we are brought up to conform and obey against our nature, we are all wounded. To heal those wounds we need to be able to stand on our own feet, centered. Sometimes I see the whole psychiatric nomenclature as an attempt to define the ways in which people have been wounded and hungry.

Meditations are a way to engage the intuitive part of our brain to open our possibilities and allow for change toward growth and high self-esteem.

Give love to that beautiful essence of yourself
That lives in this temple we call the body.
We are manifestations of life,
And are given the wonderful gift
Of an internal spirit.

—Virginia Satir

Develop contact between
Yourself and your body —
The temple in which you live.

—VIRGINIA SATIR

Intimate Body Connection

Now as you close your beautiful eyes, let yourself come in touch with the wonder that all you had to do was to think, send a thought to your eyelids, and they closed. Could you imagine that you could be in that kind of intimate connection with all the rest of your body? Not only to send messages to it, but in return to hear the various parts of your body talk to you? At this moment ask your eyelids how they feel in the position that they are in; and listen for the answer.

And then let yourself come in touch with your breathing—and behold, another miracle. Effortlessly you take the air in and all the wonderful parts of your body act immediately to take out of that breath what your body needs. You don't have to do anything about that at all. Just allow your breath to come in and then support it, and cheer it on as it goes through your total body. The process of extracting the ingredients for your growth will be done by your body without your help, and without your guidance. You just have to allow for the air to come in.

Just be in touch, at this moment, with the feeling of allowing the breath to come into your body—breathing. And as you are in touch with the feeling of the breathing, expand your awareness to see if there are tight places in your body that require your attention. And if you find any, thank them for letting you know there is tightness, and relax so that the tension and energy leaves on an outgoing breath. And now let yourself go deep inside and give yourself a message of appreciation for you.

The Power of Your Thoughts

At this moment now, your eyes are closed. Just become aware of how your eyes closed. My voice gave out words, you took the words and translated them into an image, sent it to your body, and your eyes closed. For a moment let's entertain the magnificence of that one little act. Maybe we can see it as a manifestation of a whole set of possibilities for us: that we can be in intimate connection and contact with our bodies; and that our thoughts are very powerful in helping our bodies to respond. We know the positive, and very likely it works the same in the negative.

Now again be in touch with your body. You are the shepherd to your body, and you give it directions for how it is on the chair: how it's balanced, how your feet may be on the floor, how your spine feels comfortable. You're in charge of that.

Then let yourself come in touch with your breathing. You don't have to do anything about breathing except allow the breath to come in. Where you play a role is in the condition of your body when the breath comes in. If your body is relaxed, the breath will find its way to all the places that need it. If your body is rigid, it will limit the places where your breath can go. So let yourself now be a shepherd to yourself and let your body become relaxed, recognizing that in the relaxation you are nurturing your body and creating strength. Relaxation and breathing add up to strength.

And perhaps at this time you can think of your breath as having a color. As you breathe in, at the same time relaxing your body, watch the breath move throughout your body, through all its parts, lighting up with the color of your breath; to all the extremities, like toes and fingers and nose-tip, top of head; inside all the organs; on all the surface of the skin—all of it being fed by you through the oxygen that comes through your breath.

Maybe as you watch the color of your breath, or your breath that you've given color, you could also think of a metaphor for your breath, making it possible for that breath to do its wonderful work. Maybe it's a little airplane you send throughout yourself. Maybe it's a set of wonderful bells. I don't know, but let your breath and relaxation and your shepherding have a metaphor. And maybe you can give yourself permission to let that metaphor become a part of your awareness for the rest of your life, to remind you where your strength comes from. It comes from your breath, from your relaxation, from your body, and from the power of your thoughts.

And let yourself become aware of those times and places within you when your breath is trying to reach someplace that isn't yet relaxed. It might come in the form of a little tightness—places you've noticed before—a shoulder muscle, a kneecap, your ankle, or some other place that often is tight. Perhaps you can give yourself special permission and awareness to feel that part more, because maybe it needs it. That will mean that you give attention inwardly and talk to your ankle or kneecap and send energy through your breath. You might even want to touch that part of your body and carry the loving messages from your hand to that part. And perhaps also you don't have to wait for a part of your body to ask for attention. You can just give it. Hug yourself a few times a day, pat yourself, hold yourself. Give yourself love.

A Message of Love

Let your beautiful eyes close and let yourself be in touch with your breathing. And maybe this morning even more than any morning previously, you'll think of your breath as your link to life. And therefore give yourself permission to let your body be receptive and relaxed so that your breath reaches all parts of you, as though your body were a very willing receptor to every bit of your breath.

Your body's relaxation is under your control, and it is made up of your awareness of how you allow it to relax, and how you educate your body to relax. And as you do, unite that with your physical experience of feeling your body relax. Also get in touch with your tension, which is easy to do. As you sense your tension, bless it, because it is telling you where it exists and is giving you an opportunity to allow it to relax. As you listen for the signals of tension, feel the signals of tension and allow them to relax. As you let them go out on an outgoing breath, you create a new receptive space for your breath.

And perhaps as you take in your breath you can begin to feel that it reaches way down to your abdomen and very gently fills your whole body. You don't have to push it or pull it. Just allow for the receptivity of your body, and allow the breath to come in. Relaxation and your breathing add up to strength, and it is strength in the sense of being centered.

When you add to that a conscious awareness and message to yourself that you love yourself, that message is a way of nurturing you and is another way to add strength and wisdom to yourself.

So let us hear, inside, your messages of love to you—messages of value, of caring, of connectedness with yourself. Know that your body is always willing to hear your messages of love and contact.

11

For many of us, as we were growing up, our body was only something for us to keep clean. Now you have an opportunity to really become aware of this beautiful resource, your body. Messages from your body are meant for you; you are its shepherd. Your body will try to obey you at all cost, even toward helping you get sick. Few would consciously give that message to themselves. However, if we are not in touch with our breathing, are not loving ourselves, it could easily add up to ill health.

Now go inside and see if there are any tight places. If you find them, smile at them. This is another part of loving yourself—to be in touch with what's happening. And perhaps now you can make the connection that loving yourself adds to the nurturing of you, which adds to your strength. In your strength, you can develop wisdom, health, and centeredness.

Perhaps at this point we can again become aware that our spirits are pure. Our essence is pure and is always ready to show us its purity if we are ready to listen. Despite all the messages to the contrary, of the past, perhaps we can at this time think of all those negative messages as comments on behavior and not comments on our worth.

Your Humanness and Your Divinity

Allow your eyes to close, and give yourself permission and time to go into a meditation—perhaps only for thirty seconds, but make that a part of your daily life. Become aware that as you do, you also make it possible to develop and increase your strength, remembering that as you make your body relaxed—and you are in charge of it—your body then becomes receptive to the breaths that you so effortlessly take in. Breathing in is effortless. Allowing and creating the receptivity in your body to relax is what makes it possible for the breath to do its work. Perhaps we cannot do too much in the way of helping ourselves to remember that our body functions best in relaxation. Not only does it function best, but this also makes it possible for us to be strong.

Now check. Just check all over your body for any places where there is tension. And from now on, perhaps you can regard the message of tension as a love message from your body to you, saying in effect: "You're keeping me too tight." I do not believe your intention is to make your body suffer. If it is suffering, it is not because you will it that way. So maybe you can again become even more aware that tension from any part of your body is a message, or a cry for help from your body. And the first thing is to acknowledge it, whether it comes from your toes or your knees, your neck or wherever. Have a feeling of thankfulness that you can hear your body and your body can inform you.

Perhaps you could give yourself permission to think often of being in touch with your body during the day, seeing to its relaxation and again reaffirming for yourself that relaxation and breathing add up to strength. So if you really wanted to do something very challenging, you could prepare for that by relaxing your body and being in touch with your breathing. Your will may also function more effectively coming from a relaxed body that is in touch with breathing.

This morning give your breath a color. And as you give directions to your body to relax and feel it doing that, watch your breath, with the color you have given it, nurture all parts of your body. Maybe this morning you could also put a little bell on your breath so in case you don't see it you can hear it as it moves throughout your body—a little bell, tinkling along with the color of your breath. And maybe this morning pictures may also appear. Perhaps you're sailing around in your body in a little boat or flying in an airplane while listening to the bell and watching the color as it moves. You could.

Now let yourself go deep inside and give yourself a message of appreciation for you and be aware that what you are appreciating is your life force, which is untainted and pure, and a reflection of your divinity as well as your beautiful humanity.

Life is given to us, it is that which allows this wonderful temple called "the body" to exist. Life force creates life, and breath is the manifestation of being alive. We are co-creators of ourselves. We are given life to begin with, and as a shepherd to ourselves we co-create what happens. That means we have the delicious, wonderful opportunity to be responsible, meaning we can guide. Since all the responsibility for using ourselves is in our hands, we need not fear static from the outside, because we're in charge. We're in charge of our relaxation, of what thoughts we have, and of what feelings we experience and act on. All is within us.

And so at this moment, can you again give yourself a message of love and value? You are the shepherd of yourself who is, day by day, learning how to hear from yourself, so that you can move in this world in a way that manifests your humanness. By now you must be aware that humanness and divinity go hand in hand. Perhaps at this moment, too, we can make a differentiation between our worth and our behavior. To the degree that we accept our worth, we can be more friendly to our behavior and change it when needed. We are not attacking our behavior, but rather supporting our self-worth. And that in turn will give us the opportunity and motivation to guide and change our behavior.

Being Centered

Of all the things we know in this world, we still know only a little about the essence of human beings. So much is before us, so much is behind us. So much is right here.

Now let yourself be in touch with your breathing and again note that as you breathe you make your body receptive. You are in charge of any tensions within your body. You are in charge of letting them loosen. You were in charge of creating them. You are in charge of loving them. So at this moment as you take in your breath, which carries marvelous ingredients to your body, can you now make your body more receptive to the breath coming in? And notice that as you relax your body, your body wants to take in even more air. Putting together breathing and relaxation equals strength and vitality—the strength to become centered, and the vitality to enjoy it and appreciate it.

I wonder if you could at this moment remember an incident, maybe yesterday, when you felt tension that might have been expressed to you in the way of a blame or a disappointment from someone else or yourself. Perhaps you are able to recall that state of tension. And as you do, become aware that you are able to breathe into it, to center yourself, to give yourself a message of appreciation and watch the tension evaporate. I hope this process has happened to you many times. I hope it will happen to you many, many, many more times: that when the tension is there, you will know about it, be able to acknowledge it, appreciate what it's offering you, and let it relax.

Now move to that place deep inside and give yourself a message of appreciation for you. And perhaps as each morning passes, you are more and more aware that as you appreciate yourself and value yourself, your relationships and the things you want come more easily. There are many things in this world for which we need the intelligence brought about by our centering, and the insight brought about by appreciating ourselves and it, allowing us to make decisions that will be useful in changing what needs to be changed within and in the world. We need strong, sensitive, centered people.

Changing Through Acceptance

Very gently, with your eyes closed, start moving parts of your body. Just move them gently.

Again, let yourself be in touch with your body and its comfort—your neck, your back. Gentle movement. Lifting a shoulder a little, let your toes move in your shoes or wherever they are—little movements—and see what happens. And very gently now, move your body slightly as you would like to have it move, giving yourself a message of appreciation for you. See what the words feel like inside: "I love me, I value me," and know that what you are talking about is the essence of you. Recognize that, as you give yourself more love, you then have more strength and courage to deal with those behaviors which you would like to change, and you begin to neutralize the old messages of rejection or potential rejection. Give yourself permission to remember this.

Again be in touch with your breathing and become aware that today is another day. It is built upon yesterday, and yet it will not be the same as yesterday. Those things which were started yesterday, which waited to blossom until today, can use this day for that development. And this day can also be a time when we introduce new things, because life is always pregnant with growth—always—sometimes, though, at different rates and levels. So, when you feel like it, gently let your beautiful eyes open, look around, and be aware of self, context, and others.

The Relationship Between Mind and Body

Close your eyes and think about that for a moment. A thought in your mind, directed to a part of your body, resulted in your eyelids closing—it just happened. Think of the difference between that instruction from your mind to a part of your body, and your mind sending you the message, "Write a letter." Your mind gets the message and transforms it into an outcome. When the mind does not accept the message, it will not transform it. So for the moment, let yourself be in touch with that wonderful mind of yours, and remember that it is extremely adaptable. However, it has its limits. The mind is the place where if you're really not in touch with yourself, it will reject or accept the message on the basis of your self-worth.

This morning, because this is a loving context and it is based on health and growth, my message to close your eyes was accepted by your mind. If you didn't think it was safe, you might not have closed your eyes. Your relationship between your mind and your eyes would be the same, except your mind would not allow you to accept the suggestion. Perhaps if you were threatened, you might go through the motions of closing your eyes, because you have that capacity, but it would be very difficult to do. All of this manifests the exquisite relationship between our minds and our bodies and the outcome, including the physical, emotional, and intellectual levels.

Just be aware now that your mind is like the gatekeeper to yourself. In your mind reside all the conclusions, interpretations of the past, the freedom to comment or not to comment—they're all held there.

And now let yourself be in touch with your total body relaxation. Again your mind plays a very important role. Let

18

yourself utilize all that you know about relaxing. Then, going inside, do a little survey in your body. Look for little tight places, and if you find them, let them loosen while smiling at them for letting you know. You can have a mental picture of your body relaxing, and that mental picture can become you and your relaxed body. Fill yourself with breath and relax, creating space for that breath to do its work. Then give yourself encouragement and validation by saying, "I love me, I value me."

And perhaps we can add, "I love me and value me because I'm a manifestation of life. My essence is pure, my education may seem or may have been a little incomplete or even a little wrong, but my essence, my life force, is pure. I never need to worry about my foundations. My foundations are pure, and they are the same foundations found in every human being in this world."

We all came into the world on that foundation, but many of us learned things that denied the beauty, the wisdom, the growth, the goodness of our foundation. Now we can reclaim it. We can know what our truth is. Our truth is that we are perfect beings capable of continuous learning and knowing. We don't always need to bother getting rid of one thing before adding another. We learn by adding, adding to what is, and once we know that, we can continue to add for the rest of our lives. Adding and using what we add puts that which was present into the background, and slowly it atrophies by disuse. We can just let it go and concentrate on what fits.

Go deep inside.
Find that treasure—
You.

—Anne Banmen

You are unique,
You are like everyone—
Different.

ANNE BANMEN

Your Uniqueness and Essence

Now again be in touch with your breathing. Just notice it, don't push it, don't pull it, but perhaps what you can do is give your body more messages for relaxation. Take this moment to move around inside your body and find any places that seem to be tight. And if you find them, smile at them because they're letting you know they need you. Relax them and let the tension go on an outgoing breath.

And now to move even more deeply inside and give yourself a message of appreciation for you—you, a manifestation of life, unique—there's no one else in this world exactly like you. Yet everyone is the same as you in many ways and at the same time different from you in many ways. That includes your family: the one you grew up in and the one you may be in now. You are not duplicated anywhere else in this world.

So at this moment as you give yourself a message of appreciation, become aware that you are unique. You cannot be compared to anyone else unless you hallucinate. You cannot really be competitive on a deep level unless you are misunderstanding life. You are unique and as such you deserve every courtesy, every opportunity of valuing and validating yourself, because you are a manifestation of life.

And perhaps at this moment we can begin the discrimination, the differentiation between you as a manifestation of life—perfect and pure in your essence—and your behavior, which may not be all that pure. Your strength comes from recognizing your purity in your spirit, and it helps you to form an alliance with the rest of yourself that might want to change things, or add things. That's where our strength comes from, from that alliance between ourselves and our essence, which in the final analysis is spiritual.

Connectedness with Self and Others

Allow yourself to become
Intimately connected
With all your parts.
So free, to have options
And to use those options
Freely and creatively.
To know that whatever
Was in the past,
Was the best that we could do,
Because it represented the best we knew.
It represented the best in our consciousness.
As we move toward knowing more,
Being more conscious,
We also then become
More connected with ourselves.
And in connecting with ourselves,
We can form connections with others.

—VIRGINIA SATIR

Your Centeredness and Congruence

Let us add to our awareness by going deep inside and giving ourselves a message of appreciation for us—for the spiritual manifestation that we are. And perhaps, being so closely connected to and accepting of our spirituality, we can also begin to become aware of ways in which our behavior, our communication, may not always reflect our basic wonderfulness.

We've had a long time in this world learning blaming, placating, super-reasonableness, and irrelevance. Once they were the only ways that we knew to survive. And perhaps as you come in touch with yourself, you can allow yourself to become fully aware of when you may be using any of these coping stances. Because somewhere deep inside you know that on some level, these kinds of communication, from a small way to a big way, are destructive. At the very least, they keep you from the fullness of your being. Human beings are remarkable in their ability to adjust. So many of us have learned to live with ways, little or big, that are destructive to us; and we say, "that's life." We get used to things.

Perhaps you are aware that what you learned in the past can help you become aware of how to be congruent. It is not another way to please someone, but it's a way for your body, your soul, your spirit, your thoughts and feelings to play together in a harmonious way.

See what it feels like this morning as you give yourself a message of appreciation. Perhaps the earlier voices that came, reminding you of all the ways you didn't measure up, are fainter because you now know that as you come to love and value yourself, you will be able to love and value others.

Maybe one of the most important tests we have is what happens when we face people who are blaming, placating, or being

24

super-reasonable or irrelevant. Are we now able to respond in a congruent fashion? Do we know how to do that? If we do, is it available to us when we need it? It is not hard to do what we would like when there is no stress. When the stress comes we have an opportunity to test our own centeredness and congruence.

I wonder now if you could imagine yourself internally hugging yourself, hugging that precious spirit within you? And let yourself become aware of when your spirit is asking you for help. "Please don't hold me so tight. Please don't give me extraordinary things to do. Don't ask me to move with you when you are doing destructive things, because I don't want to. Be open to me, I'm here for you." And a wonderful part is that this whole dialogue has no one else involved.

Sometimes we behave as though the dialogue isn't within us, as though it's between us and someone else. We call that projection. It was something most of us had to learn as children, because by ourselves we were helpless, and if we could project on others we could get some sense of strength. But it really never fit.

As you go deeper now, giving yourself a message of appreciation, could you by any chance see yourself surrounded by light? Light that comes because all the circuits are connected, and the light shows color and warmth and is able to help other people see it also. Now imagine yourself with the light around you being warm and bright and colorful, and you, inside, are harmonious. The rhythms of your body are working together. And in a very positive way, you are a sight to behold. Can you see that? Can you see how your facial muscles are relaxed, how your body is healthy? The next time you look in a mirror, imagine yourself flowing inside in a good way. And outside, the lights in their beauty and warmth are reflecting your inner comfort, your inner harmony.

And perhaps at this moment you could also give yourself a message that nothing outside of you that is negative is worth responding to negatively—nothing. So maybe at this moment your self-care is embodied in your ability to be congruent. It has the least destruction in it—actually it has none, but it may have pain, the pain of recognition.

Now I'd like you again to become aware of the wonder you are: your body, your mind, your feelings. Just be in touch with the wonder of you, and the many ways that parts of your body are connecting with each other, sending information back and forth (for instance: among your immune system, your endocrine system, and your neurological system). Information is moving, of which you really have no awareness. We are a veritable mixture, an interactional mixture, of continual information moving within us, and also moving between us and someone else. So as you now come to another awareness of your beauty, of your magnificence, of your complexity, also become aware of the imposition that many of us have made on ourselves naively.

You cannot find anything in yourself that is not already there. So the excitement, interest, and enthusiasm for allowing yourself to mine the gold in various situations and relationships and learnings, are all found within you. Now remind yourself that you are a human being of the universe and therefore have access to the energy from the center of the earth with your groundedness, and from the heavens with the ability to have intuition, to be connected with people outside of you.

Now let yourself be in touch with what thoughts and feelings arise as I have led you into different aspects of looking at yourself. If there are one or two aspects you would especially like to work on, to know more about, let yourself know that. Maybe when the meditation is over you can write them down somewhere. Now again be in touch with your breathing, with a message of love to yourself. And then see if you are willing to send energy to the outside for people in need of it—without strings. And when you feel like it, let your beautiful eyes open, and give a special awareness to what it feels like to go from one place to another, from closed eyes to open eyes, to moving. And if any sounds or other movements want to come out, just let them happen.

Your Light

Let your light
Shine forth from
Your temple—
Your manifestation
Of life.
Let your light
Illuminate your path
And enhance your destiny.
Bathe yourself in the glow
Of your internal spirit.

—ANNE BANMEN

Learning Is Infinite

At this moment perhaps you can become aware that your learning potential is infinite. It is not stopped by age or sex or color or education. It is a part of your heritage. Your ability to learn is infinite. What may stop it is a feeling of low self-esteem, and that is only an idea, not a fixed reality. Now let yourself be in touch with your breathing and see if you can, each time I ask, be in touch with your breathing just a little bit more—more aware of the breath as it moves within you, as you offer your relaxed body to receive it.

Now let yourself go to that place where you keep the resources that are called by your name: your ability to see and hear and touch and taste and smell; to feel and to think; to move and to speak and above all to choose. And to realize that these are your prized, precious, wonderful resources that will take you everywhere—to every unknown place you want to go. You are equipped to move there because of your resources.

And then become aware that house-cleaning is often in order. What worked yesterday may no longer fit today. Perhaps after a time you can let it go and create something new for what you need at this point. Needs and wishes change as you move in this world. So to keep yourself up to date with what you need now, look at what you have. Use that which fits; let that which no longer fits go with your blessing. Give yourself permission to add that which you need which you yet do not have. And since you have infinite possibilities for creation, you can always find what you need.

We are manifestations of life,
Pure in essence and containing
The most powerful ingredient
That exists in the world: the power to grow.

—Virginia Satir

Make "you"
The center
Of your own
Existence.

—VIRGINIA SATIR
ANNE BANMEN

A Unique Being

I accept that I am a unique being
With similarities and differences
To every other person.
There is no one exactly like me.
All the courtesies, love, and energy
That can be extended to any other human
I also give to myself
Because I am a unique being
Worthy of appreciation and high self-esteem.

—Virginia Satir

You Are Unique

Perhaps, today, as you contemplate giving yourself a message of appreciation, it feels more and more natural for you to think of yourself appreciatively, without reference to any other human being—knowing that you are a unique being with things in common with every other human being, but in no way do you add up exactly like anyone else in the world: not your mother, your father, your sisters, your friends.

You are unique, and as you go more comfortably toward allowing yourself to accept your uniqueness, and allowing yourself to give appreciation to you, feeling it is a natural, normal thing to do, see what happens to your body. Does it smile inside? Does it feel like a smile or relaxation wants to come out? Just be aware.

Most of us are new to the idea of appreciating ourselves. And now go to that place deep inside where you keep the treasure that is called by your name. And as you move to that place, comfortably, notice your resources—your human heritage.

What Is

Increase your willingness
and consciousness
about looking first
at what is.

—Virginia Satir

Using Your Resources

Going back to where you were
Is a lesson in defeat.
Going forward is an experience
Into the unknown,
And going into the unknown,
You go safely
As you rely on your resources.

—Virginia Satir
and Anne Banmen

To Be Grounded, Inspired, and Connected

Now go to that place deep inside where you keep the treasure that is called by your name . . . your name. As you go to that special place, look at the resources that are there: your ability to see, to hear and touch, taste and smell, to feel and to think, to move and to speak, and above all, to choose—to choose out of all of that, that you have at this moment, that which fits you well, for this NOW. Allowing all the rest to be there, comfortable, but not in use.

Again, be in touch with your breathing. And let yourself go with your attention to the center of the earth, where the energies flow constantly and move up to your feet, ankles, legs, and into your torso, bringing the energy of groundedness—your ability to be related to your reality; to be relevant to the things and people around you—your energy of groundedness.

Then allow yourself to go to the heavens. Feelings of inspiration, imagination, and intuition move and join with the energy of groundedness, forming still a third energy—the energy of being in contact with your fellow beings, the ability of communicating—moving out through your hands and arms and fingertips to people outside of you, giving to and taking from those others.

Our feeling of worth, our presence on this planet is based on the ability to be grounded, inspired, and connected.

Intellectual and Intuitive Resources

Now again, to remind ourselves of our resources: our ability to see and hear and touch and taste and smell and feel and think and move and speak and choose. These are your companions with which to go into the unknown. And perhaps at this moment we can be reminded that as we move about the world and respond to what we see that reminds us of something that once was an occasion to feel helpless, we no longer have to move to that helpless state. We are not helpless.

So at this moment we can give ourselves strength and awareness to be in touch with the fact that the past has already gone and that nothing in the present that triggers the past will ever make the past come back, unless we recreate it by being helpless in the moment. We are now big, we are not children. We see, hear, touch, taste, smell, feel, think, move, and speak from our own insides, not at the direction of others, if we so choose. We can move to the point that no matter what triggers from the outside, it may trigger pain, but it does not take us off our center.

We are receptors of energy from the center of the earth, which gives us our ability to be cognitive, to talk intellectually, to talk concepts. And we receive energy from the heavens, which allows us to use our imagination, our intuition, our inspiration, and which truly gives us the basis on which we enter new ground, by sensing, by intuition, by trying it out. And this energy together with the energy of cognition forms a bridge to two vast reservoirs of resources for our use: that which comes intellectually and that which comes intuitively. And these two resources together, as they contribute and blend, add a third power: that which allows us to move from the inside to the outside, with that which we are

36

extending to others who are ready and who have their receptors available.

In the past we were living under strict rules: men under rules not to be in touch with their soft side, their sensing side; and women under rules that they should not be in touch with their logic and their ability to think. Now we know these are two parts that belong in each being. Thinking and feeling, yin and yang, soft and hard, belong in both. We become whole people as we allow ourselves to let both those parts grow, and in so doing, create for us a solid base from which we can go to congruent relationships with people outside of us. We do not ask them to be our softness or hardness, and we do not permit them to use us in that way.

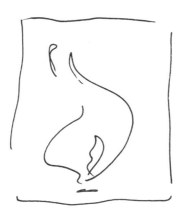

The Life Force of the Universe

As we give love to ourselves, we give ourselves permission to feel and to relate to our deep life force. As we connect ourselves with our life force, we no longer have to be shy and think we are selfish, because all we're doing is acknowledging and manifesting our relationship to the total life force of the universe. We are essential links, each one of us to each other. And as we come in touch with our feelings of value for ourselves we can openly say to ourselves, "I value me, I love me." One of the wonderful outcomes is that I will not have to ask you to do my work for me, but instead, because I am loving myself, I can love you.

And just for this moment be in touch, as deeply as you can, with what you feel like when you say, "I love me, I value me." For many of us it used to be: "You can only be valued if you do the right thing." But now we know if we value ourselves we can become a team with that wonderful energy within us and create anything we want in the world. Anything.

And then we can remember our resources that we carry with us everywhere. These make it possible for us to go into the unknown equipped: our ability to see and hear and touch and taste and smell, to feel and to think, to move and to speak, and above all to choose—to choose out of all of that which we have at this time that which fits us well—we have a lot. And to let go of that which no longer fits, blessing it because once it did fit. And then to notice that which we need yet do not have, and to give ourselves the permission and the courage and the creativity to develop it. That's a process we can do for the rest of our lives. And in that process is the secret of vitality, and our growth.

Also remember that as beings in this universe, we have access to the energy from the center of the earth which brings us our

38

groundedness; and to the heavens, which brings us our intuition. These are there for us to use at any time. We are all really part of it. Our job is to know it and access it. When we do, we create the third energy, which allows us to move out to those on the outside who are ready. Not those whom we desire should be ready, only those who are.

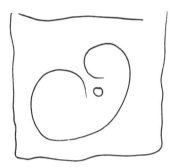

Choice Points as New Beginnings

Gently close your eyes, get in touch with your breathing, and allow yourself to relax. Perhaps you could even do it more fully as you become aware that to relax your body is to create strength for you. And give yourself a message of appreciation. Recognize that appreciation for you is for the essence of your life, which given in large measure gives you the support and the strength to change that which you want to change about yourself.

Now go to that place deep inside where you have your resources, those resources that will carry you everywhere: the ability to see and hear and touch and taste and smell, to feel and to think, to move and to speak, and above all to choose. And recognize that your resources can be continually enhanced, enabling you to see more clearly, more deeply, more fully; hearing beyond the words; feeling, in all its dimensions; thinking as broadly, as deeply, as comprehensively as possible; moving in many ways that are new: moving with your body, moving with your awareness, moving with your skills, moving and recognizing that movement and breathing are important parts of ourselves; and speaking: to speak the unspeakable, to speak the up-to-this-point-unknown, to speak with words that have color and sound and passion and reality; to choose, recognizing that a choice point is like a new beginning.

Structure Enables Us

Structure is for enabling at a moment in time.
Not for yesterday but for now and tomorrow.
And we could take that even further—that when
We have structure that enables us in the present
We go toward the future in a more centered way.

—Virginia Satir

Feelings of Value

This morning as we begin our meditation I'd like you to be in touch with the awareness that it is your essence, your spirit, your sense of self, your value of yourself that is your safety—that is your source of growth, that is your source of connectedness. Your valuing yourself is the basis of you being integrated as a whole being. Everything else is a variation of your particular theme. How old you are, what color you are, what things you've done in the past, what hopes you have—they're all variations of the theme. The basis of you and me is our feelings of value about ourselves. Our self represents a manifestation of life, and therefore our valuing of ourself is the valuing of all life everywhere.

I try to keep my eyes on how—in all ways I know—to help you to learn to value yourself, to be in touch with the magnificence that is you, and to make the separation between your magnificence and your behavior, because your behavior does not represent your magnificence. It represents what you have been taught, and what you have learned, and how to cope.

There is only one way that new human beings can come upon this earth, and that is through the meeting of the egg and sperm that are present in males and females. We call those people our parents. The most important thing in all of that is that the sperm and egg met and completed a seed which grew into us. The people who had the egg and sperm were showing us by their behaviors, with each other and with us, what they learned—not what our value was, or even theirs. We can now become aware that the most important thing is that they were the vehicles by which we came into this world. And the next most important thing that could happen is that we see ourselves and them as pure beings, knowing that is the truth.

We are living in a time when for the first time in the world this is possible. There are opportunities to see ourselves in different ways than ever before and to know that we, as manifestations of life, purity, and divinity, are connected to all life, all over the world.

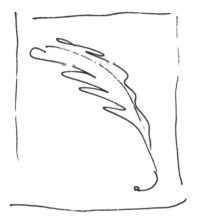

Let Music Touch You

Let your attention go to the music and just feel the music as it enters your body. Let your full attention be on it. Maybe you can even feel certain parts within yourself responding to the music. If you can feel it, imagine what particular part of your body this music is touching, and see what happens as part of your self is touched. What happens to the other parts? And also be aware of any feeling you have on your skin as the music moves around you and within you.

Find some place where you can begin to make a rhythm of your breathing. Simply focus on it. Don't push it, don't pull it. Just be aware of a rhythm and combine the awareness of the rhythm of your breathing with the feeling of the music.

And now let yourself give yourself a message of appreciation for you. See what it feels like as you say deep within yourself, "I appreciate me, I love me." Go back to the first time you did this. See if this time it feels different, broader, deeper, more energized. Maybe you are accepting that as you grow to love yourself, you will not have to diminish others or project on others. You will not have to fend others off, because as you grow stronger in yourself you become more creative about handling anything outside of you.

Life's Beginning Brings Joy into Your Life

Now allow yourself to go back in time, whatever that time may be, to when you were a part of the energy of the universe—present, but in the form of pure energy—a part of the power of the universe. And as you moved along, the spirit within you asked for a new form. And as you moved into that form, in the many shapes that it took, you found yourself here on this planet, as a baby. A baby who, without your conscious knowledge, came for a special reason that you have long ago forgotten. And as you go inside the body of the woman who carried you, while your new form was being perfected and shaped, let yourself become aware of the wonder of a form fulfilling itself.

You came in the form of a seed—two seeds joining. And day by day things moved so that, phase by phase, you began to fill in the form that you would become: a human being on this earth, on this plane. Day by day, something new developed, something you needed as a piece upon which something else would be built. And little by little during that time you became the form that was to be yourself as a little baby. You came from the place where you were into the new place, being quite aware, in ways in which you could be aware as a baby, that you were continuing a wonder-journey that would take you to new possibilities on this plane.

You came fresh, you came whole, you came with awareness, you came with substance, you came being blessed as a manifestation of life. You came being able, because of your human endowment and your spiritual base, to become joyful, creative, efficient, loving, real, healthy, and happy, and with an ability to love yourself and to love others. You also came with the possibility of having thoughts and ideas that could effectively cut you off from all your potentials. You have the freedom of choice—choice to use what you have.

Let yourself have a picture at this moment of yourself as you are emerging from the birth canal, this wonderful miracle that occurs, called human birth. And then look at yourself as you were able to sit up, to walk, to run around, to talk, to create all kinds of things: fantasies, art, and new possibilities for yourself. That beautiful biological clock within your body took you through the stages of development such as adolescence, and moving on to your full growth.

The wonderful essence that you were once a part of transformed itself into something very specific. You have a special name that means only you. You have a special look that means only you. You have a special way to walk that means only you. You have special tastes and wishes that mean only you.

And I wonder at this time if you could give yourself permission to reawaken to all the levels that are open to you at this moment— your possibilities for flowering. Your "self," a wonderful, fully evolving human-being! Give yourself permission at this moment in time to know that whatever there is, there's more to come.

Now as you see yourself, know that you are bringing many, many experiences into the present. Each experience helps you deal anew with whatever your present brings you. You are filled with expectations, knowledge, and conclusions, all of it having been gained through your journey up till now.

So as you look at yourself, allow yourself to see a true manifestation of human art. And then give yourself permission to notice what about yourself you would like to be different. Give yourself permission to find ways to achieve that which you wish for yourself, whatever it may be. Perhaps at this moment you can be aware that life is a continuum of developing something new.

And now let yourself go forward ten years. Look at yourself and see if there is anything, as you look at yourself, that you could say then you wish you had done. Allow yourself to listen to that information. Store it away somewhere. Perhaps it will have use for you in the present.

Now go ahead twenty years and again, as you look at you, is there anything you would say to yourself, looking at you twenty years from now, that you wish you had done before? If so, use it as a resource for your present. And also as you look, notice your beauty and your possibilities.

And now move on to the moment before death. You are ready to leave, to move into another consciousness. And as you look at yourself at this moment, what would you say about what you hadn't done? What would you say about the joy in your life? What would you say about your beauty? And whatever it is, could you make it information for the present for things you might want to act on?

And then as you let yourself be aware that at some time you again will join all consciousness, be aware that the moment for our living is NOW. A NOW that can encompass all possibilities. A NOW in which you can feel and think and see and hear and choose.

Manifestation of Total Integration

Sitting relaxed in your chair, allow yourself to be totally taken over by the music. Whatever wants to happen, let it happen; whatever thoughts, feelings, sensations, pictures, just let it happen. Be aware that you are giving inner expression to something that is coming from the outside of you through your pictures, your thoughts, and your feelings.

Now, in a moment, give yourself permission to add an outer expression. It might mean you want to stand up and move. Let yourself gently move into adding the outer expression. And while you are doing this, just become aware that an inner response and an outer expression are the same. Just let come what comes. When an inner response matches outer expression, you are in total charge of you and in full reception of all your power. There is nothing to separate you from it.

Perhaps you can become aware that the big word is *choice*. You can choose these states. You can choose your inner response. You can choose your outer expression.

Very, very gently let your body come to a comfortable, still position: not rigid, just still. And in your mind's eye, project a picture of yourself outside of yourself with inner response and outer expression matching. Now look at the expression on your face, then give yourself permission to live in that state as much as you want.

And perhaps the next time you are by yourself or you want to be by yourself, you'll turn on a little music and repeat this experience, choosing music you like but picking it for different moods, and remembering that when inner response and outer expression fit, it's the manifestation of total integration.

And now let yourself become even more comfortable in your chair, and again allow yourself to receive the music. Note whatever pictures or feelings come up. And as the music gently fades, let yourself go to an awareness of your breathing and message of love and value about yourself. Give yourself permission that as you go toward infinity, you can experience all you want.

Now check inside your body for any places that may be tense, and notice those places that are really very relaxed. Smile at both places as you go by, for each is telling you something important. Now, feeling yourself totally centered and relaxed, let yourself send energy to whoever you would like to in the universe.

And now allow yourself to come slowly here, greeting yourself gently, gathering awareness as you come back. When you're fully here, let your beautiful eyes open. And again, if any movements or sounds want to express themselves, let it happen.

To Choose and To Be Aware We Choose

When we become aware of our learnings, we are describing and connecting with the persons who were our teachers from birth. Whether we call them that or not, they were the models from whom we learned how to be in this world. Many of the modelings that we've had somehow seem inappropriate, but we don't know what to do with that. At the same time there was much in the modeling that helped us, or we wouldn't be here today. So it's important to realize that the basic modeling all of us had enabled us to be here. The difference may be that we paid a higher price than we need have.

Now we can move in new directions to continue our lives from this point without having to pay a high price. Remember, we are here, we got here, and what we are now into is a life without such a price. Another way of stating that is: we don't have to sacrifice ourselves so much to live. Be aware right now of any thoughts or feelings that come. As I say, we no longer need to sacrifice ourselves to live. We can learn other ways to live.

And now again, become aware of what we always have with us: our resources—our ability to see and hear and touch and taste and smell and feel and think and move and speak and choose. All of these were given to us because we are human beings. These are our resources that take us anywhere we go. Therefore, wherever we go we are always well equipped. Our job is to access and connect with and learn to use these wonderful resources.

Without knowing it, many of us have blocked the ability, temporarily at least, to see clearly because of fear, to hear correctly because of fear. Perhaps at this moment in time we can be aware that using our wonderful resources to see is the beginning of new sights, new sounds, new tastes and touches and thoughts. It is another road to strength.

And also become aware of that very special ability we have to choose at a moment in time, to choose consciously. We are always choosing, but we are not always aware. Now as we raise that wonderful ability of choosing to the level of consciousness, we know that it is the "I" at this moment in time that is choosing. Whether I do it to please you or to avoid pain or punishment, I am still choosing. And as I become aware that I am making the choice, I also add strength to myself.

And now again become aware that this is a constant process that we can engage in: letting go of that which no longer fits, adding to ourselves that which we need which fits better, and honoring that which we have at this moment in time which fits us well. Each day, each moment as we learn, we can let go of that which no longer fits, with a blessing because once it fit us well.

Now again, be in touch with your breathing, and maybe at this moment also be aware of your miraclehood. We are all miracles, miracles of life and being. And your job is to connect with that miraclehood. To be the kind of shepherd that allows the miracle to unfold. And now also remember your connection with the center of the earth, which brings your ability to be grounded and logical and cognitive. And your connection with the heavens, which moves downward through your head and neck and face into your chest, and brings with it the energy of inspiration, intuition, imagination—that part which gives color and texture to your life.

And as these two come together, they create a third energy which allows you to move from the inside out to those who are ready to receive you. And to those who are there but are not yet ready, send your loving light and move on. And as you do this you also work toward developing your strength. When the receptors and the senders are open, the connection is made. You cannot push it, you cannot force it, you can only enlighten it.

The Ingredients of Our Internal Process

Far in the background are the strains of music. Just let yourself be in touch with the sounds that come from that music. Now let yourself be in touch with your breathing in a conscious way while the music is present. And perhaps you can become aware that the sounds of the music are within you, reaching receptors that may be there in various parts of your body. Your breath is coming in; and if you give your body permission to relax, your breath can do its job very well.

Maybe at this moment you can also become aware that you are a receptor to many other things. The world, the environment where you live and work and play, and the people within that environment are sending out messages. The planet sends them out—the earth and the mountains. We send out, we receive. And the forms that we take in, and that we respond with, are different. A sight is different from a sound. A touch is different from a sight. A sound is different from a thought. These are all ways that we connect, that we send messages back and forth. We have a wonderfully responsive body. We also have a body that can focus itself to send out things as well as receive things.

Perhaps you can become aware that by developing more and more awareness, more and more connection with your body, you can be in intimate contact with it. And that you may be able, for instance, to become aware of what is around that you may or may not want to take in. You may become aware of things within you that you may or may not want to talk about openly. You might become aware at this point that if you do not really get in contact with yourself, you may be doing things behind your own back, such as sending messages you do not intend or responding to messages that aren't even happening.

A metaphor for me is that I am always in the center, with all kinds of things coming to me and going from me. Anyone in my presence is receiving something, and I'm receiving something from that person. Whether it's harsh words, loving words, a kiss, a touch, a sight—I'm receiving. I'm also giving. For many of us this whole set and source of communication has always been going on; but it has eluded us.

Perhaps now is the time to re-introduce ourselves to that which was our only means of giving and receiving information before we had speech—the touch, the sound, the look, the act. Perhaps we can allow ourselves to become aware of and willing to look at all kinds of ways that we communicate with one another that have nothing to do with words. Let's allow ourselves the freedom to explore these kinds of communication.

I would like, at this moment, to provide you with a thought: that ever since you were conceived you have been involved in communication—giving and receiving—but probably there wasn't anyone there to code it for you. So perhaps you can give yourself another chance to recode, to understand the meaning in ways that are different from what you understood before, through that wonderful world of making contact that is beyond words. This is not to say that words are not important. They are, but there is so much more.

Now let us move to that place deep inside where we keep our resources. I'd like you to become aware of all the ways you have to observe with your eyes, what you see. At this moment you are probably aware that what you see has to be run through how you interpret, and how you interpret is run through your past experience. And what you can say about it has to be run through your rules for commenting. While you may be aware of what you see, by the time you get the words to someone else, it will not have the same meaning. Could we take the time, then, to allow ourselves to share as fully as possible what we see? This also means sharing how we interpret and what permission we give to share completely, beyond the rules.

Another part of our ability to observe comes through our ears. We hear through those wonderful organs. We take in, but this too needs to be run through the same things: interpreting what you hear, running it through your past experience, and running it through rules for commenting. What is left comes out of your mouth. The same is true for touching, smelling, and tasting.

There is so much as we truly allow ourselves to observe and put meaning to our observations. Perhaps at this moment we can be very much aware that what we see at first glance covers the interpretation, the past experience, and rules for commenting. Unless we know how to ask the other questions, or to put them out, we cannot really connect with another person. It is natural for all of us to try to interpret what we observe. It is natural that we give meaning from our past, because our future is not yet here and our present is only forming. And given the way most of us have been brought up, it is natural for us to run this through our freedom to comment.

I'm adding another dimension to observation by looking below the waterline of the iceberg, looking beneath the words. This may be a new place for you. What you tell me you see tells me also that if you are interpreting something, it belongs to past images and is run through your rules for commenting. If I take everything you say at face value, then I run it through my interpretation, my images, and my rules for commenting. So what happens is, I understand you through me. That's what projection is all about.

Now here we are at this moment with these wonderful ways to observe, and getting more and more understanding of what may be behind these observations, of how we can separate me and you so we can truly find you and me. Now we're into the most creative part of our communication. Let us also remind ourselves that we feel and think, using our organs for interpretation, before we take action. Our action follows as a result of what we have done, and following this through is where we can learn that we are always doing the best we can. Looking a little differently, interpreting a little differently, becoming more fully here, and giving ourselves messages to comment openly, the results will be different.

Now let yourself be in touch with the meaning of what I have just given you. It has many parts to it. Whatever is going on at a moment in time in your reality will be the outcome of these stages of how you observe.

Now let us go to choice, which may at this time be something you are more and more cognizant of: that you have choice points at almost every step of the way, and your choice is your ability to direct what you are doing. It moves you from any victim space to a space of dignity—your conscious choice.

And so now at this moment again, let us be in touch with the wonderful resources we have, and give ourselves the permission to do the sorting that we need to do every day, every week, every month—looking at what we have, what conclusions we've made, what past experiences we're using, and what ways of commenting we are using. If we no longer feel that they fit, perhaps we can let them go, and let them go with our blessing. Perhaps once they fit us well. And now we look at what we have that fits just fine, and also notice that which we need, which we do not yet have, giving ourselves permission to create it. This is the essence of life reflecting and unfolding itself.

We Are in Charge of Ourselves

We are in charge. We are in charge of how and when and in what way we take in our breath. We are in charge of how we see ourselves and how we are with ourselves. What we aren't in charge of is whether it rains, whether it snows, whether somebody yells at us, whether somebody criticizes, or whether somebody loves us. We really are not in charge of that, only of how we respond.

When our bodies and our hearts and our minds are in harmony, we send out positive energy which attracts other positive energy and also acts as a way of softening the anger and the negative energy within our sphere. To that degree we influence what's happening by our own harmonious energy.

It's been shown that crimes are usually not committed in sight of people when it's light. When it's dark, more negative things happen. And the darkness is like looking at negativity. So become aware that we are automatically a light in any darkness when we are harmonious with what we think, what we feel, how we are, and how we love ourselves. And that light grows ever brighter when we know absolutely, crystal clearly, that we are manifestations of life, and that we are pure in essence.

Your ability to create
Is based on your ability
To choose.

—VIRGINIA SATIR
AND ANNE BANMEN

Creating an Internal Process of Value

My eyelids are closing, and as they close I feel myself creating another context. It's the context within me, inside. As I leave the context from the outside, I am no longer aware of your eyes and your body, but only aware of mine. I have the feeling of consciously creating a context in which I want to do something special.

The special part is to give myself, internally, attention, respect, and love. I create the conditions to do this by letting my eyes close and being in touch with my bones, the physical balance between my body and the chair, and my feet on the floor. And further, to create the condition of receptivity in my body, I allow myself to respond. All of these are under my specific direction, and therefore are tools for me to create what I need to create.

So as my eyes are closed, I give my body directions for relaxation and then allow myself to be aware and give attention to my breath. And as the breath comes into my body, which I have given directions to relax, the breath fills my body with nurturing ingredients. As I tentatively open up the spaces, my breath eagerly goes to those spaces, and I feel a sense of calm and a sense of peace and, simultaneously, a sense of strength. I know I will go on breathing even when my attention is not there. But like me and everyone else, my breath too likes to have a special time for attention—to be thanked for being there.

And now I go deep inside to give myself another thank you, a thank you to me, the manifestation of my life force, and my feeling of value about my being that manifestation. I recognize that I am the shepherd of what will happen to that life force by how I think, how I feel, how I act, and what I do. Again, I realize that I'm in charge of the fate of myself.

At this time as I become aware of myself and as I consciously give a message of appreciation to me—which could sound something like "I love me, I value me"—there is another thing that happens. As I love myself, I create the context in which I can love and value others. I can put space between me and old, early learnings that you and I are separate and that you and I are either bad, good, right, or wrong for each other. You, too, are a manifestation of life, and I can open the way for a connection with you by how I revere and feel about myself.

As I come in touch with how I value me, I have a new sense of being kind to me, of doing things that will be helpful to me. If I have any habits that could injure me, I can marshal the courage to change them, because it is all in my hands. So as I come in touch then with my feeling of value about myself, I can also be in touch with my wish to love, to help myself grow, and to put myself in a condition wherein as I meet you, I meet you at the highest level and feeling of value. Then I am more able to separate your life force and mine from our behavior. I can also do what is necessary to change my behavior.

And I do not do this alone, for I have been given wonderful things. I would like to go now to that place where I find my resources—that wonderful place, that sacred place where I notice my ability to see and hear and touch and taste and smell. These are my basic resources for taking things in. To feel and to think, which are my inner resources for processing what goes in. And then to choose.

In addition, too, remember that I have taken many actions and spoken many words, and my words and actions have fit what I felt and thought, and were related to what I saw and heard and touched and smelled. It is all together. So at this point in time, my ability to choose allows me now to take out of all the things I have learned, those that fit me well at this moment, and those that I have developed. However, when I look for something I need, I may find that I don't have it. Therefore I know, as I reach for my resources, I have what I need to develop that which I want.

As I scan my psychological closet looking perhaps for the things I need and want, I may notice things that haven't been used in years or very clearly are no longer fitting for me—old rules, old concepts, old conclusions that now, with a little wisdom, I know do not fit. I want to honor those things but also allow them to leave. So I let them leave with my blessing, to go wherever old things go. It leaves room in my psychological closet for new things.

So I'm in the process of adding to, of letting go, of connecting with—a process that goes on forever. And in that process is vitality and the freedom of life to unfold itself. As our needs manifest differently and as we move along, our wishes expand. So we need a way to allow ourselves to keep abreast of what is happening. A wonderful, wonderful way is to take psychological inventory periodically of what is there, what fits, what fits well, what doesn't fit, and what is needed.

Recognize—
    That you are
        The source
            Of decisions for you—
                You are the sole decision-maker
                Of your internal process.

                        —VIRGINIA SATIR

As we become more conscious
And allow our choices
To become more conscious,
We will move in the direction
Of growth.

—VIRGINIA SATIR

Making Choices that Fit

As we look at our resources, be aware and appreciative of all the things we have seen and heard, felt, touched, and smelled, all the thoughts and feelings that have been a part of our life up to this time, all of the choices and the words and the movements.

We have a great resource from which to choose. And because we have chosen one way in the past does not mean we have to continue that way, but it could be one of the choices when we add other possibilities. As we come fully in touch with our capacity, inborn in all of us, to choose out of all we have at this moment, that which fits us well, we notice that there are things we haven't used. Once they were very fitting, but now we can clear them out, sending them on their way with a blessing for what they did at that time. No longer useful are thoughts such as, "I must never share my feelings or you will be hurt." Maybe at one moment in time that did fit, but maybe it will never fit again.

If you were to find many things that you learned and no longer have any use for, could you allow yourself to choose to let them go with your blessing? Once they served you well, but now they are no longer necessary. And could you look at what you have that fits you well? Honor it and give yourself permission to add to yourself that which you need or want but which you still do not have.

As you allow yourself to look again at your resources, become more fully aware that they are there for your constant use; that you are the one who selects not only what you will use, but how you use them. And could you, while you are doing this, also give yourself permission to let go of everything except the experience you can use for learning, that will make your present *illuminated.*

Risk Something New

At this moment, experience the precious NOW. Look at what you have developed as each moment fits well for you. And give yourself permission to invent that which you need which you yet do not have. Depend on your resources: your ability to see and hear and touch and taste and smell; to feel and to think; to speak and to move and to choose.

Becoming aware that there is much that is already there that you may not yet have attended to, give yourself permission to risk something new. And perhaps you can also give yourself permission that daily, weekly, or monthly, you will allow yourself the sorting process. It can be called learning, it can be called growing, it can be called rejoicing. It can be called manifesting joyfully your life force, in your present physical form.

Making Room for New Possibilities

Now let yourself be in touch with your breathing. And I'd like you to go to that place where you keep the treasure that's called by your name, which has all the resources you need for anything you want to do. These will take you anywhere, change anything you want: your ability to see and hear and touch and taste and smell; to feel and to think; to move and to speak; and above all to choose—to choose that which fits for you at a moment in time. Looking at all you have developed, notice now that which fits you well. It has stood the test of time, and it grows ever more useful to you.

However, there are also things in your psychological closet that you have outgrown, that you don't need anymore. Once they fit you well; for example, if you hadn't been stubborn when you were growing up, you wouldn't have made it. Maybe you don't need that any more, at least in that form. Could you allow yourself to look in that psychological closet, as you come to choose something for yourself, and notice that which no longer fits? Perhaps it brings back a smile of recognition or one of pain. It was useful to you in some way. Can you now know that it is time for it to leave, and let it go with your blessing?

All the old rules that have been transformed—could you now let them go with your blessing? They helped you to get where you are, but now they are no longer helpful. Bless them and let them go. Old attitudes that you may have had and now experience in a new light, that no longer fit—can you let them go, knowing they were a product of another time when it was the best you knew? Now you know something better, or you see clearer, or you see more, so those old attitudes no longer have a place in you. Bless them and let them go.

And then can you look, as more psychological room is made in this psychological closet, at things you want and need, that you yet do not have? And give yourself permission, because of your resources, to get what you need. You can learn what you want: your body will cooperate. Remember, your body is extremely sensitive to thoughts. Age plays little part in all of this, as you well know. So as you look at what you need, the room in your psychological closet is present now, because the old things that no longer fit have gone, and you now have space for the new.

And maybe at this moment you can let yourself be aware of one such thing that now looms ahead of you, that feels like it draws you, that it beckons you . . . something you'd like—like a new skill, a new love, a new possibility, a new way of being. Look at it, and let yourself know that you have everything you need to accomplish it, not because you will it, but because the positive energy that moves from you will help you create the form in which you can attract what you need and want if you give yourself permission. There is no age limit on this either. There is no sexual, racial, political, or religious impediment except what you might put there.

As you attend to the budding and the flowering of you, the only one exactly like you in this whole world, see ahead the new possibilities. Add to that which you have now, knowing that you can do it because you have resources, because you love yourself, and because you are the recipient of energy: energy from the center of the earth, which gives you groundedness; from the heavens, which gives you your intuitive, imaginative parts and your ability to relate to people outside.

And now move again inside to the resources that are called by your name. Go to that treasure house deep within and notice those resources. These are the resources that will take you everywhere: your ability to see and hear and touch and taste and smell; to feel and to think; to move and to speak; and, above all, the ability to choose. Recognize that any choice, at any moment in time, represents other choices that could have been made. You choose the one that fits the best for you at this moment. You could say that those you didn't choose you lost, and that may be true. What you choose is a gain, and if that doesn't work you can always choose again. Your ability to choose—to be able to say no to one thing and yes to another—is that which fits you, not what fits somebody else.

Recognize that we humans are in a sense like little pack rats, because we keep everything that has ever happened to us. All those experiences go into our psychological closets. And as we look into our psychological closet for something we need at a moment in time, we may find something that was useful a long time ago—perhaps when we didn't know any better, or when it was the best we had. So we can let it go with our blessing, thus making room for the new, because surely as we move on we will need new and different things. We have the resources that can provide them. So our closet is forever being looked at in terms of what is no longer fitting, what fits us well, and space in our closet is for us to add that which we yet do not have. Being able to be in touch with this, we keep abreast of our own vitality and growth. In addition, we can remember it is a part of our heritage of being human.

Choice gives us the opportunity to change directions. At any point we can activate choice, Choice also represents the opportunity to let some things go, in the interest of adding something different. As we get in touch with that wonderful skill or facility to choose, which is also a way of looking at life, we can become aware that the choices we make go into our psychological closet and are there to be used again if they fit. And if they never fit another situation, we can let them go with our blessing.

Each choice is a creative act which may or may not ever be used again. And so, remembering that even if you let something go that you no longer feel is useful to you, at any point you can create something that will work for you. Your ability to create is based on your ability to choose. At this point you can see ahead the many choices that can come between now and then. Each choice can carry you to a new place in your life.

If you make choices that go forward, as in the glass that is filled halfway, your choices can reflect the half full rather than the half empty. Life wants to move ahead, never backward, for to go backward is working against the stream. Going back to where you were is a lesson in defeat. Going forward is an experience into the unknown. And going into the unknown, you can go safely because you carry your resources.

So at this moment you can become aware of many things that have happened, many ways in which you have seen more deeply, heard more clearly, touched more significantly, and noticed your choices—all the things you had an opportunity to do. And now you are aware of the new clothes in your psychological closet. Maybe at this moment you can allow yourself to think of something that was not there before but will now give you an opportunity to move forward, opening doors as you go, deepening, broadening, and at the same time helping you to be clear about what fits.

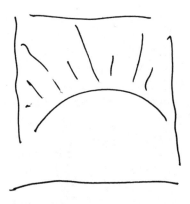

Create the Image of Yourself

Let your body relax, and start a journey beginning with your toes, feet, ankles, calves, knees, thighs, hips, genitals, and stomach—all your inner organs—chest, arms, shoulders, neck, head, and all the parts of you. Give yourself a message of appreciation for you.

I would like you now to put an imaginary movie screen in front of you. On this screen I would like you to project yourself as you would like to see yourself. This movie screen also has sound, so project onto that the sound you would like to have, the way your voice sounds, the way you move, and how you look. Just put that image out and notice your healthiness. Notice your ability to express yourself, your laughter and tears—sometimes in anger or frustration—whatever it might be.

Now look even more carefully at what you've projected and give yourself permission to accomplish your image, because that will be an expression of you, and you can actualize that image. Notice this has nothing to do with how much money you should make or what job you should have—none of that, but simply how you look and sound, how you sparkle, how you move, how you speak, what your body looks like for you.

Look again at this wonderful image you're creating and ask yourself if what you see is really what you want. Sometimes we ask for things that we aren't all that sure about. Just look, because maybe you aren't projecting fully enough. Maybe you're not going as far as you might. The universe is limitless, and our ability to reflect that is also limitless.

Now on this screen, could you add another person, and watch yourself as you respond, as you connect with, as you appreciate, as you are real with that person, whoever it might be—someone new

69

or someone you already know? Maybe you can visualize yourself in creative conflict management, having intimate experiences, feeling open and vulnerable in a good way, learning between you, or having healthy competition in fun. Know all the time that it's only fun—teaming up together to create something, being able to be in the presence of someone else and doing what you need to do at that time, and seeing that the tyranny of togetherness is no longer there, but rather happiness and fulfilment in each of you doing what you need to do, coming together when it fits, planning, dreaming, and being together when it fits.

Now tune in to your own body. What's been happening as you've watched the movie you have just created, a movie of you which represents your images of how you can be? What's been happening to your body? What's been happening in your feelings? What's been happening in your thoughts? What was happening in your heart? Maybe at this point you can give yourself permission to know. As you let go of the things that get in your way of manifesting your image, the image then can actualize itself.

When I talk about you giving yourself a message of appreciation for you, contact that deep place and realize all you can be, because you are a manifestation of life with limitless possibilities. Now let yourself know the resources you have—still looking at the movie, still watching yourself. Notice what you are wearing and so on, but know you have all the resources right now to go for it—the ability to see and hear and touch and taste and smell; to feel and to think; to move and to speak and to choose.

And because you are privy to all the energy in the universe, you receive the energy from the center of the earth, which brings you groundedness—the ability to think and reason, forming strategies and plans for things; and the energy from the heavens as it brings you your ability to be inspired, to sense—your intuition, your connectedness with the information and wisdom of all time; and the energy from those persons outside of you with whom you can connect, whom you stimulate and are stimulated by. You've tried out so much, you already have a tremendous amount of experience. You have found things that work and things that haven't worked. You don't have to do the things that don't work anymore.

70

Now give yourself permission to think ahead three days hence, and look at the movie and see yourself three days from now. Visualize yourself as a being of magnificence who has been through some experiences where some things have been added, and perhaps some things have been let go. See yourself three days from now—being. Just notice it, and then look ahead a week from now, one week from today, when you may be in a different context. See yourself in your own integrated way, feeling whole, feeling good, feeling in charge of yourself. And see yourself six months from now, aware of where you might be, what your context might be. How do you expect you might be?

Could you give yourself permission six months from now to go again through this experience with yourself, to look at new images of how you would like to be, and use your wonderful resources to go for it? You have those resources. Then could you see, stretching far ahead of you, a road of continuing life, vitality, discovery, and new possibilities? You have all that it takes.

Through Chaos Toward New Integration

As you look at all that you have at this moment, give yourself permission to develop that, to acquire that, to practice that which fits for you but as yet has not become fully a part of you. Like any other learning, we are always awkward when taking new steps. We will pass through the chaos part. The awkwardness, paired with our patience, our courage, and with our sense of direction, will gradually become a part of new integration. And once achieving that, we will again feel the wellspring within us to go farther.

Allowing the Impossible to Happen

We are at the eve of knowing the potential of our ability: to commuicate with others, outside of words—communication on the level of sensing—not only with those close to us, but with humans all over the world.

Once upon a time, it was only a ridiculous, impossible idea that human beings would find themselves on the moon. However, that is no longer a ridiculous, impossible idea. It is a reality.

It was once thought impossible that we could sense one another in a really clear way and send messages back and forth. More and more people are aware that we can send information and energy between people who are in each other's presence, or who are outside of each other's presence anywhere on the planet and maybe even in the rest of the galaxies.

And maybe one of the things that we can allow ourselves to do, fully aware of any skepticism we may have, is to begin to affirm what we would like to have happen and allow ourselves to take the steps to make that happen—not pushing, just allowing it.

Building on yesterday's experiences, allow your senses from both your logical mind and your intuitive mind to become aware that there is much more than logic. I think there's much more.

See what it feels like as you give yourself a message of appreciation for you. Perhaps as you appreciate you, you feel in yourself many new parts, many new possibilities, and even more knowledge. You have more to appreciate. What does that feel like when you say, "I appreciate me, I love me"? Maybe along with this is the awareness that to the degree we love and appreciate ourselves, we will no longer have to make other people do it for us, and we can begin the wonderful process of enjoying others and loving and enjoying ourselves. In that way, we come together on the basis of attraction and not compulsion.

Your fears
Are only manifestations
Of familiarities
Of the past.

—Virginia Satir

Your past becomes a light when it helps you to
Notice what's going on in your present.

—Virginia Satir

Developing Your Self-Esteem Maintenance Kit

At this point I would like to give you your self-esteem maintenance kit, which I hope you will receive, accept, and become familiar with using. The first thing in this kit is a detective hat, which you put on immediately when there is a puzzle or a question or an effort to understand, "How do the pieces fit together? How do you explore for the gaps and find the things that fit?" This is in contrast to judging. Many people judge before they explore, but I would like to recommend to you that you keep your detective hat handy for any time a question, a puzzle, or a gap appears, so you can go on a journey of exploration.

The second thing in your kit is a medallion, which you can hang around your neck. On one side in beautiful jeweled letters it says, "YES." Underneath that "YES" it says, "Thank you for noticing me. What you ask of me at this time fits just fine. The answer is YES." And on the other side in equally beautiful jeweled letters is the word "NO." Underneath, it says, "Thank you for noticing me. What you ask of me at this time doesn't fit at all. The answer is NO."

This is the key to your integrity. Yes and No are both loving words. When you say yes and you feel no, or when you say no and you feel yes, you have eroded your integrity and weakened yourself. So keep your medallion fresh within your awareness, and always say the real yeses and the real nos—keeping your integrity intact and keeping your strength strong.

The next thing in the kit is an empowering wand, a courage stick, a wishing wand. All three names can stand for the same thing. And when you feel a wish or a desire to move in a direction, you can take this empowering stick in your hand and move, dragging your fears behind you if they're there. If you wait until all your fears are taken care of, you probably will never move ahead. As you take that empowering wand, wishing stick, courage stick in your hand and move forward, many times your fear will have been dissolved by the time you reach where you want to go.

To take this wand and use it to empower yourself means you use yourself as a reference: Does it fit? Where do I want to go? You are the one who sees the vision. No one else can see the vision, and many people—not knowing your vision, not understanding it—will try to dissuade you because they think that you will be hurt. Many people do not trust going into the unknown. But with your vision to guide you and your hope to guide you, you can move there—and most of us have to go alone. Or, if not alone, you cannot be dissuaded by the people around, who out of their fear try to dissuade you. The growth in all of us is strong and wants to have continuing new expressions. And so your giving yourself per- mission to move in the direction of your visions, of your dreams, of your hopes and wishes is what brings you to new growth levels.

The next thing in the kit is a golden key. The golden key enables you to open any door, ask any question, make speakable what is unspeakable, and attempt the undoable—to make it doable— opening up the possibilities, looking in all the cracks, noticing even the smallest kind of movement. That's your golden key.

The next thing in the kit is a wisdom box. The wisdom box is part of your heritage; it's part of what you came into the world with. For me, I have located it by going into my navel two inches and going up toward my heart. Halfway between I find the wisdom box. This wisdom box is in contact with all the wisdom of the universe—all the wisdom of the past and all of that which resides within you. It is that part which you sense sometimes giving direction, sometimes called the still, small voice. It is that part deep inside that knows and tries to give directions. Like a thought or a feeling, you will not find it on a surgery table. You won't find the wisdom box there, but I don't question the presence of a wisdom box. It is that part of us, when we are cleared of all our defenses and all our fears, in which we can hear the stirrings of our growth and our wisdom. Perhaps our greatest job in life is to remove all that stands between ourselves and our wisdom, and then to recognize that all human beings have a wisdom box. It needs only to be tapped.

Look again at your self-esteem maintenance kit: your detective hat to explore, your medallion for your integrity, your empowerment stick to go straight to your vision, your golden key to look at anything, and your wisdom box to be in touch with the wisdom of the universe. Your body is the manifestation of the universe with all it contains.

Let yourself now be in touch again with your breathing. And if those tools are not already within your grasp, or you have not already used them, could you give yourself permission to try them on for size and let them become yours?

As you make more use of your wisdom box and all of your tools, you can then go into your psychological closet to examine what is there for you, what you need right now. And you may find that there are things there that came about as a result of your saying yes when you felt no—which might include anger, rage, or resentment. Or you may find things there that have said to you in the past, "You don't deserve to go farther, you have done bad things." But you will recognize this for what it is—a misunderstanding of you and yourself. And as you clear your closet of those things by sorting them, by noticing them, and by letting them go, you can make room for new things that come as a result of new ways of viewing yourself.

Opportunity for new visions and ways to get there is enhanced by your connection with the center of the earth, which brings energy upward to your feet and legs and gives you groundedness—the ability to think, to know, to collect knowledge, to be reasonable. And also you are a recipient of energy from the heavens, which moves downward through your face and neck into your arms and torso, bringing with it the energy of imagination, of intuition, of sensing—the kind of thing that gives color and song and texture to your life. And as these two come together, they create a third energy, that which allows you to move from the inside of yourself to the outside, where you can connect with those eyes and ears and arms and skin and ideas that are ready and open. For those that are still in bud form, not yet ready, allow yourself to notice, love, and pass by.

So this morning, as you come into this day, give yourself permission to know that your underpinnings are solid; that you are a wonderful, magnificent being of this universe, and you have only to learn about that magnificence.

And now if there is anyone in this world, including yourself, who would need energy from you, anyone you want to send it to—world leaders, family members, friends—take this moment to send energy from yourself. Send it with a love message that says, "Use this as you can." Then very gently let your attention come fully here and gradually open your beautiful eyes, looking comfortably around. And if any movements or sounds want to come out, just let that happen.

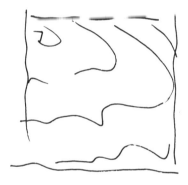

Using Your Detective Hat

Your detective hat is a special part of your self-esteem maintenance kit, to be put on at any moment when you need to learn something, when something goes wrong, or when there's a puzzle. Put on your detective hat rather than reaching for your judge's hat. Many people judge before they've discovered anything. But in your self-esteem maintenance kit is your detective hat. Give yourself permission to use it frequently, because you will need it frequently. The moment you reach for it and put it on your head, you have great powers for discovery. It can help you remember to turn your awareness to observing, both with your eyes and your ears—to discover what's behind something. Perhaps you give yourself even a fuller awareness that what is apparent at a moment in time is like the tip of the iceberg, with so much supporting it that cannot be seen. That's why you need your detective hat. Now, in addition to its form and its color, give it a quality of texture. Feel the special fabric it's made from.

Give yourself a message now, that forever after, for the rest of your life, you will put on your detective hat before your judge's hat. Chances are very great that if you put on your detective hat, you may not need your judge's hat. Take a moment now to put the hat that you have just created into your hands. Look at it, feel it. Maybe it makes little sounds as you move it. Listen to it. And remember, you created it—it is just for you. Now you can place that hat into your self-esteem maintenance kit.

The Medallion of Choice

The medallion is to help remind yourself that you can look at anything, listen to anything, but swallow only that which fits. The meaning of the medallion is, "Yes, this fits fine. No, this doesn't fit at this moment in time." And now both yes and no become gifts, gifts that help you stay in harmony. "Yes, this fits me well. No, this doesn't fit me, it's out of harmony with me." And as you use these two words and their meaning as gifts for yourself, you are also giving gifts to others. You are keeping your flow of harmony, which is the most powerful force in the world for good and for nurturing.

So at this time now, let your beautiful eyes open and gently bring yourself fully here. If there are any movements or sounds that want to come out of you, let it happen.

Responding Instead of Reacting or Controlling

Again, be in touch with your breathing. Don't push it, don't pull it, just be aware of it. And now go further, deep inside to that place where you keep the treasure that is called by your name. As you approach this very sacred place, let yourself notice your resources: your ability to see and hear and touch and taste and smell; and to feel and to think, to move and to speak; and above all, your ability to choose. You can choose out of all of what you have at this moment, that which fits you well and you want to use because it fits.

And then, looking at that which you have which you no longer need, but which once fit you very well, allow yourself to let that go with your blessing, because once it did fit for you. Like a garment in your closet which once was wonderful but now you've outgrown, let it go with your love.

And then look at what you need which you do not yet have, and give yourself permission to acquire that and to develop that. And as you allow yourself to be in touch with this sorting process, be aware that it has gone on since you began in this world and can go on until you leave. Choosing is something only you can do.

Perhaps uses for our detective hats are now more obvious to us. We can see more times when we can use our detective hat rather than our judge's hat. We can be conscious of our integrity by our "yeses" and our "nos," and know that "yes" has nothing to do with love and "no" has nothing to do with anger. It has to do with what fits: our root to integrity.

And then move to that sacred place again, remembering our resources: our ability to see and hear and touch and taste and smell, to feel and to think, to move and speak, and, above all, our ability to choose. Know that we carry within us the ability to respond by choice to whatever is outside of us.

No one can legislate our choice. However, we cannot control that which comes from outside of us. We could not control our mother's temper tantrums. We could not control our father's depression. We could not control our older brother's wishes to take our things. We could not control our mother's laughter, we only responded to it. Many of us have been brought up believing that we control the outside. We do not, but because we were brought up that way, we didn't learn that our job, privilege, and responsibility were to choose how to respond. In that choice and in knowing we have those choices is our centeredness. That means that we do not use the outside to define us. The outside is just a source of information, as I am to you. And whatever I give, whatever I show, if it fits some place in you, then you can have it. And if it doesn't, you can just let it go by.

Let us look now at our psychological closet and notice those things that once fit us very well, or at least helped us to survive at one point, but no longer fit. We can begin the process of taking them out of our psychological closet, blessing them for what they did, and now letting them go to create room for that which is new. It is important to bless all the things we let go, because once they did something for us—something we needed at a moment in time, or thought we needed. Things that are blessed go more easily than things that are hated or condemned.

Our blessing lies in the fact that we can always create new things. The past does not imprison us, unless we allow it. So here we are: a new day, new possibilities, looking into our psychological closet and letting things go that we no longer have any use for. We are looking at and honoring what we have that fits us just fine at this time. And we are looking forward to creating that which we need and want but do not have, knowing without a shadow of a doubt that it is all possible—to let go that which is not needed, to honor that which we have, and to create that which we want and need which we yet do not have.

Could we again become in touch with our power of choice? Knowing that at any moment we have the choice to be in touch with our breathing, with our feelings, with the feelings of someone else. And give ourselves permission to elevate that wonderful power within us called choice. When we engage in choice, all compulsions recede. When we change compulsion to choice, choice brings new strength.

Now could we remind ourselves again of being able to be the recipients of the energy from the center of the earth, which brings us our groundedness; and from the heavens, which brings us our intuition? These energies are always there. We need to remember and access them; they will never go away. Our groundedness allows us to be centered. Our intuition allows us to be creative and to know.

At any moment in time, live beings that we are, we can connect with people on the outside who are ready. We cannot connect with anyone who is not ready. All we can do is shine our light. And maybe this is a time for us to remember that our ambition may cut off our opportunity to see when the time is ripe. We may be, without knowing it, asking people to abide by our timetable and holding a subtle threat if they don't. Maybe we can let that demand go and know that life is always going to manifest itself when it is nurtured and when it is free to choose.

And now again, let yourself be in touch with you, and be aware of any thoughts or feelings that come to you—new ones, perhaps, that you haven't thought or felt before. And if anything is coming now that has a special meaning, let yourself notice that. Many mornings ago, I woke up with the thought, "You cannot direct the life force of a violet." Maybe something is coming to you which has a deep meaning, such as that thought had for me.

I'd like to remind you that we are capable of infinite possibilities and we live in a time now when it's possible to develop those. Fifty years ago it couldn't have happened, but it's happening now. So at this moment would you allow yourself to send energy to any of those people in the world that you know about that need your energy? Include yourself if you like, and give the energy without strings—a pure gift for those who receive it, to use as needed.

And then let yourself gradually come here with your awareness in this room, making the transition now to be more outer than inner focused. Take your psychological time to come back over the bridge from inner to outer. And when you are here, open your eyes. And if any sounds or movements want to come out, let that happen.

Manifesting Your Dreams into Reality

Now at this moment, I would like you to be ready to receive a symbol, a symbol that I will give the name "wishing stick"—a magic wand, a courage instrument. You will find in that instrument—that symbol of your courage—your ability to move ahead, to manifest your dreams into reality. It takes courage to do that.

As this stick, this wand, comes to you, take it firmly in whichever hand you ordinarily hold things. And as you pick it up, give yourself a message to endow this stick, this wand, with your courage. In one hand you carry your courage, which takes you toward your dreams. In the other hand you may want to carry the feelings you have, which include your fear, your hesitations, your love—all of the human feelings. They will not need to get in the way of the manifestation of your dreams.

As you grow in your familiarity and your ownership of your own courage, with whatever feeling you have in the other hand, you may find that your courage helps the feelings to be transformed: your fear into caution, your hesitations into looking around to see what next steps to take, and your love into manifesting strength.

So at this moment, with your wishing stick, your symbol of courage, your magic wand, your gateway to your dreams and a manifestation of those dreams, let yourself think of a dream. It may be one you could accomplish today or tomorrow, or any dream you have that you would like to start on. And perhaps as you hold this stick, this wand, you'll give yourself permission to use the courage that you endow it with, to make your dreams a reality. Perhaps you can picture that dream already accomplished. What does it look like? What does it feel like? How do you feel as you see yourself in the dream already accomplished?

Now give yourself permission to take the meaning of this manifest symbol into yourself. Perhaps for a while you might want to carry this wand with you as you deepen the meaning within yourself. And now give yourself a message of appreciation for you, and permission to use yourself in whatever new ways you need to accomplish your dreams. Again be in touch with your breathing.

In a moment, feel yourself completely here, in this room. And then let your beautiful eyes open, and whatever sounds or movements want to come out, let that happen.

Move Ahead

And now again be in touch with your self-esteem main-tenance kit. As you become even more connected with it, it will become almost automatic that you explore with your detective hat before you judge; that you are clear about your yeses and nos so you keep your integrity intact, and know that your real yeses and your real nos will add up to health for you; and that you know you have your courage stick, which always precedes your fears. You cannot wait until you are free of fear to move. It is in the act of moving that the fear begins to dissipate. With your courage stick you can reach for the stars if you want. Reach out. No one knows what they yet do not know, and to limit your future by the limitation of your present or past is to imprison yourself.

So take that courage stick, that wishing stick, and move ahead toward what you need and want, letting the fear drag behind. This will often result in your fears diminishing. And then look at your golden key—something as a child you had to watch out for: not to ask that question, not to notice this or to show that. Most of us have related that to our safety, but now maybe we know that safety really lies in knowing what's on the other side of the door, or what's on the other side of our question. To find that out we need to ask. We need to take that risk. So your golden key is really your risking.

Then be in touch with your wisdom box—that which unites you on the level of spirit with everyone else; which connects you with the intelligence of the universe, which also rests in yourself; and which is the part of you that senses what you need. The voice is often very soft, and when we're loud within ourselves we might not hear it. Perhaps you can give yourself permission to quiet yourself, to listen to that voice, to listen to what's in that box.

Your Sanctuary

I would like you to visualize a place you have been where everything was wonderful, even if it was only for ten minutes, or five minutes, or one minute. Whether you experienced it many times or only once, a place and a time where everything revisited was wonderful. Perhaps it was in your living room, on a mountain-side, at the ocean, in a wheat field . . . wherever.

Notice the color of that place. Notice the time of day. Is it morning? Is the sun rising? Is it high noon? Is it sunset? Put the time of day and the colors together. Now let your attention go to the air around you. Is there wind? If so, how fast is it moving? If it is still, notice that. And notice the temperature. Is it cold, is it hot? Is it snowing, is it raining? What's happening?

Notice the shapes of things around you. Are there shapes you call chairs, shapes you call mountains, shapes you call streams, shapes you call chickens, or people? Notice the shapes. And notice also if they're moving. If you are overlooking a stream, notice the fish. If you're on a mountaintop, notice the clouds, perhaps moving. Or in your living room, notice the curtains waving, or the little kitten moving. What's moving?

Now feel your awareness at this moment, too, that you are at a place where you've been before. And let yourself come in touch with the feelings that you have right now, being there. This is a place where you have felt complete and happy and whole. Let yourself have those feelings again. Feel them again. And let yourself move in any way that fits for you as you look at things, as you touch things, maybe even as you talk or laugh or lie down or stand up. Just be aware of your feelings where all is happy, complete, and whole. You feel confident and of value. Your self-worth is high.

Suddenly, your eyes go to a place that somehow you have not noticed before. And you feel drawn to what you see. It seems so compelling and attractive. It's attracting you. You find yourself moving. And as you move to that place gently, but slowly, for some reason you have a need to put your hand in your pocket. As you do, your fingers find themselves connecting with a key. You pull it from your pocket and see it is gold. A golden key!

For some reason you put your hand in your other pocket and there again you feel something very wonderful on your skin. You pull it out and find it's a hat with a visor. The words written across it are, "Your Detective Hat." And it asks you to put it on your head. You have it! For you, detective means to look at something, to find out something, to explore something. Again you feel the key. The key, you know, has to do with opening something.

While all this has been going on, your feet have been slowly moving in the direction to which you are attracted. By the time you have your hat on your head, you're almost in front of a very beautiful door. You look up to the top. It's huge, it's beautifully carved in just the wonderful carving that you like. Then you notice that there is a lock, and your little detective hat says, "Well now, if you put that key in there maybe it will fit." And so you do, and lo and behold, it fits perfectly. As a matter of fact, as you put the key into the door lock, it seems almost as though it's happy to be there, that the lock and the key have been wanting to get together for a long time, almost as though they are saying thank you to you for doing it.

The door, large as it is, opens effortlessly. You step inside. You see a room that is very large, high ceilinged. The feeling is so good, as if it is also beckoning you, "Come in and join in the wonder, joy, and pleasure that is here." You take a moment to let yourself take in these feelings. They're very strong. At the same time they're very soothing to you. They feel so good.

Then you give yourself permission to look around, and you notice the wood—just exactly the kind of wood that you like. You notice further the windows. Some of them are made of beautiful stained glass, in just the colors you like, with the forms and pictures on them that you like. And you notice the walls, the pictures, and colors, just exactly what pleases you. It couldn't be better. You hear music, just the music you like, playing especially for you.

You enjoy the sounds coming to your ears, the sights coming to your eyes, and the feelings that are bathing you. You know somehow that you've never really been here before, but you have imagined what it would be like: an accompaniment to feeling whole and complete and of value. And as you're taking all this in, on one level it seems very, very natural. On another level it is a big surprise.

Now you allow yourself to look further and find there are a few steps that you need to go down. As you do, you notice a large, long shelf with books on it—many books. They're beautifully organized, their bindings are pretty. And there's one book that seems to stand out, almost as though it had beckoning fingers to catch your attention. You move toward that, and as you gently place your hand on the back of the book it almost comes out to meet you. Then you look at what it says on the binding, and it says *The Book of Me*. Underneath is your name. You pull the book from the shelf. You open it. On the first page is a dedication. You wrote it, and the dedication is "To Me," and your name is underneath it. You turn to the first page and, like all stories, this one starts out the same: "Once upon a time . . ."

What follows is the story of your birth: the story of the people who were around when you were born, the story of what was happening, how people felt, how they may have felt differently from the way they looked, what they were doing, what the world was like when you came—whether it was war time, or whether it was fun time, or whatever time it was. And as you move farther in your reading, you read about the people who were your parents, or were good friends of your parents, or were your relatives.

You find the story of your parents' lives. You know information about their inside world that may not always have shown. It's a beautiful novel about people—not always perfect, not even always happy, but human, with happiness mixed among other things. You're fascinated by what you read. And you read on.

You read through your early steps: your falling down, your getting up, your learning, your new meetings. And then you find yourself coming to today's date, and the page is blank. Somehow as you get to this page, the book seems like it's a lot slimmer in front than you thought. There's so much that has not yet been written.

Above today's date, written very clearly in a script you like, in a color that you like, is, "Each day brings new possibilities. Your past is something that can illuminate your present. Detach it from contaminating your present." And you know as you look at these words that so much more is ahead of you. As you look at this book and the blank pages, you know that you will come here often to write, to write in this book, *The Book of Me,* which is YOU. You will chronicle the things that happen to you, being aware of the things that are changing, discovering more of the things that bring you joy and pleasure, and learning more about how to cope with things outside yourself. You really do know that this day is special. And you are filled with a sense of awe, a sense of infinity, a sense of possibility.

But now it is time to leave. It's easy to leave because you know you can come back. You know you can come back any time you want to this wonderful place. You also know you can read and reread all the things that have been written before you write anew. You close the book, you put it back on the shelf, and it's almost as though you hear inside a "Thank you. Thank you for noticing me," meaning thank you for noticing YOU. "Thank you for taking the time to honor me, to understand me, to love me, as I have appeared to you in the pages of my book."

You turn around. The music has changed to something you like equally well. The light has changed, and there are new lights in the room. You realize that no one else will ever come to this room. This is yours and yours alone—your sanctuary where you can go. You move out, and again the huge door effortlessly closes. You turn the key in the lock. You put the key in your pocket. And somehow you also know that having this key now, you will never lose it. You cannot lose it. It is your passport to new possibilities.

You take off your detective hat, looking at it, smiling perhaps. Your detective hat can lead you anywhere you're willing to look. And it folds up so nicely. You know also that this hat will never leave you either. With a reawakened sense of possibility and discovery of the most fantastic creature that was ever invented—yourself—you move back now to the place where you were.

You take a moment, allowing yourself to breathe and take in the sights and sounds, then gently give yourself permission to move back to the present. As you come now fully to the present, you find yourself here in this room. And when you feel like it, give yourself a message of love and appreciation and whatever you would like to have yourself remember about your journey. Then gently open your beautiful eyes and let yourself be here, and whatever sights and sounds want to come out, let them do so.

Loving the Inner Child

Let's give a message of appreciation to ourselves. Perhaps it's getting now more familiar, and maybe even in some sense easier, and maybe in another sense broader and deeper. The message could sound something like, "I love me." Maybe we can have a deeper appreciation of saying that as a message of love to our spirit, to our life force, which is a reflection and perhaps even a manifestation of our divinity.

What does it feel like to be so clear, if that's where you are? Loving yourself, your spirit, your essence, your life force, gives you the courage and the strength to look at your behavior—any behavior you would like to change to become more fitting with what you want for yourself.

You have the courage to move beyond the pull of familiarity, which we all know is strong. Our courage and our strength, which can be manifest by messages of love to ourselves, can help us move beyond that pull of familiarity and give us the courage to go into the limbo period, the chaos period, which has to happen if we are to grow.

So now again be in touch with how it feels to you to give yourself a message of love, and perhaps to recognize something else: that as you fully love yourself, you will not have to demand love from others. You can connect with others in a more full way. The yearning from our insides to be at peace, to be loving and connected with other beings, is a yearning we all have. And a first step is to love and value ourselves so that we are fully in a position to respond to people outside of us in a real and congruent way. This establishes the foundation for love and trust.

And let us now move to our medallion in our self-esteem maintenance kit. On one side it says, "Yes, thank you very much

93

for noticing me. What you ask of me right now fits just fine." On the other side it says, "No." Beautifully jeweled letters say, "Thank you for noticing me. What you ask of me at this time doesn't fit. The answer is no." So as we give ourselves permission to be real and clear and have integrity, our relationships with other people will grow. As a result we will get positive feedback. We will be able to hear the truth from someone else, we can regard that as a gift, and we can give the truth to someone else. It will be our gift to them. When we have clear-value love feelings for ourselves, we need in no way ask other people to pay for our life, rationalize it, or even justify it.

Come with me on your magic carpet to your sactuary in that special place. As you move there, let there be lightness in your heart, let there be a song in your voice, let there be love and realness surrounding you. And as you move now to the door of your sanctuary and move into your beautifully appointed room, with all the colors just right and everything the way you like it, you'll notice a figure in this room. The book is there and you will see it soon, but your eyes are drawn first to this figure. You look at the figure and you know instinctively it is your inner child.

Your inner child looks at you, and today that inner child can say to you, "I know you love me, I know you will help me, and I know now you will listen to me. And that makes me feel the courage I need to go with you into the unknown." This child is beautiful in the way you are. The child is willing to go beyond the wounds that it has suffered in the past, and it is ready for your guidance and your help. And as this child, which you know is part of you, puts out his or her arms, you reach and embrace that child. As you do that, an inner feeling of connectedness and light comes upon you.

Many of our inner children have not been nurtured by us, not because we didn't want to, but because we didn't know how. Now we can become aware that we are just a broadening, a deepening, a lengthening, and a wisening of that inner child. Our inner child is our foundation, and our inner child learned along the way the best that it knew. It is very educable, and the minute we give it new education through love and through new actions, our inner child grows.

And now you know when you come to this room, you come to make a connection in a deep way with this inner child, which is a very important part of you. So together with your inner child, go to the book that is fairly dancing to come out of the shelf to you. And as you open to the first blank page, would you write what it feels like to you to become so intimately connected with your inner child? Hear the wonderful music that is your special music, in the background while you write. And be aware of the feelings that you have while you are writing and about your experience of openly acknowledging and accepting your inner child.

Now while you are involved in writing, could you also become aware that whatever you got in your growing up was never the result of a direct intention from your parents, especially if it wounded you? It was the outcome of where they were. You had no way to know this, but now you can be educated and you can do what fits for you. You can look at it as an act of love to your parents when you do what fits for you to make yourself happy. I think you are fulfilling the wish of your parents, just as seeing your children do what fits for them fulfills your wish as a parent.

Now let us get ready to close the book for this visit, remembering we can come back here at any time. This is your private sanctuary, to meet again with your inner child, to write again in your book. And in this library, and maybe in your real library at home, will be *The Book of Me* that flows out of your maps, your family-life chronology, and anything else you want to put in it. This is your record, your account of your appreciation of yourself.

And now as you close the book and move out of this room, again with the feeling of lightness and perhaps also some memories, you lock the door, climb on the magic carpet, and come back here refreshed, comfortable, and hopeful.

A Process of Integration and Wholeness

Through loving ourselves, we create the conditions under which we can more effectively love others. I can meet you when I am fulfilled. I will not ask you to give me what I cannot give myself. I will not have to project on you that which I cannot accept in myself, because what I have is okay. I can reach out when you're ready, and I will know that or I will know how to find out, and ask you to join with me, to walk with me, to talk with me. We can do it together.

You do not come to me because I command you. You do not necessarily come because I need you, but because both of us are open to each other. We walk, and talk, and plan, and manage, and all the other things that people do—loving, crying together—because we can connect with each other through the freedom that starts with fully loving ourselves.

And to help us along the way, to keep us on track where we might want to be, we can more fully embrace our self-esteem maintenance kit. We can remember to put on our detective hat before we judge, and be able to stand in someone else's shoes as well as our own, and be able to explore possibilities. And perhaps when we come to the judging, it will be with understanding.

We can be clear with our medallion—that which helps us with our integrity to say the yeses that fit and the nos that fit. We can know that what we are after is fit and not revenge, not blame. We're looking for fit, the most loving thing to do with how we either value ourselves or others. The most beautiful dress or the most beautiful suit, if it doesn't fit, is not for us. And we do not have to blame the suit, the dress, or ourselves because it doesn't fit. It happens that it doesn't fit. You don't even have to apologize or explain. It simply doesn't fit; and we can love ourselves in the process of recognizing whether it fits or not. No matter how much I love it, if the dress doesn't fit, I can't wear it. No matter how much you love it, and I want to please you, it still won't fit.

So for our medallion, we can develop even greater freedom to check things out for size and then see. Does it fit? If it fits, the answer is, "Yes, thank you for noticing." If it doesn't fit, the answer is, "No, thank you for noticing." Our medallion is our manifestation of integrity. And as our yeses and nos fit, our sense of power, creative power, and centeredness gets reaffirmed.

And now let us look at our wishing stick, our courage wand, and realize that to go toward what we want, we put this wand in our hand, and whatever fears there are will trail behind. We can take our energy to where we want. This courage stick gives us that energy, that power to go toward our dreams and go toward our wishes. Oh yes, maybe you haven't been there before, but you have everything you need to take you into the unknown. Your fears can follow behind you.

And now become aware of your golden key once again, which allows you to look at the secrets, to look in the doors, to look in the windows, to look under the covers, to ask the questions. Wonderful! When we were children, so many doors were closed. We weren't to ask this or comment on that. Then we grew up, and our teachers said, "You are too young" or "too old" or "too fat" or something. Let it all go! If you want, just look, ask, or comment— that's what your golden key is for. And that, too, goes toward developing your sense of power, your sense of centeredness. You don't have to put any energy then into avoiding what you very much want to know.

And now let us look at our wisdom box, that wonderful, wonderful part of us that allows us to be connected with all human-kind, all lifekind, and the intelligence of the universe. As we allow that to become very freely a part of ourselves, we can begin to give up the fears of our limitation, our deprivation, our fears of punishment, and move where the energy takes us. We are part of all the energy of the plants and of the mountains. We are all basically part of nature. And as such we have something to give to each other, and it will come through the wisdom box—which has very little to do with words. It has to do with sensing what it feels like when we put our arms around a tree, or smell a flower, or hug a human being—the centeredness, the power of life touching life—and allowing the secrets of the universe to be available to us. It is possible to learn how we sense and how we know everything that has happened, on some level. When we allow ourselves, we can access almost anything. That's because we have this connection with the universe.

Now I'd like you to board your magic carpet and move to your sanctuary, enjoying the ride and the colors and the feeling of moving on this magic carpet. And as you alight, look again at this place where everything is exactly as you would like it. Reaching in your pocket for your golden key, you now take the familiar route to where the door beckons. You move toward it. The key opens the lock very easily, and you are again overcome with the beauty and the fitness. Everything here fits you: the music, the colors, the wood, the form, the light, everything.

As you move to that bookshelf and take the book, you feel a tugging at your waist from a little arm that goes around you. You look down and find it is your inner child, now happy, now knowing it has a wonderful caretaker—you. You reach down and embrace your child, and together you take the book. As you read the new page, "You and Your Child," you write together of what will be the next steps you take. There's nothing between you now that can separate the two of you. You know nothing will come between you in helping you laugh, heal your wounds, or pursue your dreams. This is a moment of integration, of wholeness.

You write about what you are feeling right now about you, and what you see as new possibilities. You write confidently, comfortably, feeling perhaps somewhat awed, but you write. And when you stop writing, it's like a pause for you, because the next day and the next day and the next, you can come back. You are in the middle of the process of becoming what you will probably always be—in the process of "becoming more fully me," more fully manifesting your humanness.

As you put the book back, you carry your child with you, knowing you are a loving person to your child. You feel whole and strong, knowing that feeling whole and strong means that whatever happens, you will have the resources to cope with it and not have to be defined by it. You move out of the sanctuary feeling light, perhaps with a song or a joke, remembering, "Of course! I'm a cosmic joke. I can laugh at me, but I can do that because I also know I'm a sacred being."

You lock the door and board your magic carpet to come back. As you alight, coming here, you have with you your love of yourself, your kindness and lovingness to that inner child, and your freedom to use your self-esteem maintenance kit.

And I'd like you now, if there's anyone you'd like to send energy to, including yourself, to allow that to happen. And when you feel like it, let those beautiful eyes gently open. Feel your whole body as your eyes open and your attention comes to what's here. And if any sounds or movements want to come out, let them.

Finding Your Own Path

And now, very quickly, move to your sanctuary on a high-speed magic carpet. There, in front of your door with your golden key, you open the door. And now inside you feel the beauty—it's just as you like it. You move to the bookshelf and take out the book, *The Book of Me*. It has your name on it, and you open it to the page of today.

You look at the last sentence from yesterday, which could have been the last conscious thought you had before you went to sleep. Now you start today's page with: "What did I learn yesterday that will be a new foundation for my life today? What did I learn? What did I learn that opens up something new for me—that validates something I knew before—that is something very new, but I know it fits? I know that it fits from my own wisdom, not because somebody told me."

As you're there, writing in that wonderful book, which is your own private possession—never to be seen by anyone else unless you show them—feel what it feels like to begin to have a more conscious relationship between you and yourself. Take yourself fully into your consciousness and let yourself be fully connected with you. After all, you are the shepherd of that wonderful being that you call by your name. And let yourself have permission whenever you want to go to this place and write in your book, writing with a pen, writing with your memories, writing with your pictures—whatever you write with.

Perhaps, at this time, you might write in your book a wish you have for something you would like to have happen. You may have the help of others if you ask, but it's your design. Perhaps you might now become more used to thinking about, "What do I want to have happen for me?"

Know that you can make the design, and then look for how you can implement it. Maybe you'll only get part of it made, and you'll make the rest as you go along, as though you were forging a trail in a place that never had a trail. One step ahead—see what's there, to the right or to the left, whichever seems to have the most space. You couldn't have mapped that ahead of time, and maybe that's how it is with us when we go to the unknown: We take a step, and then we see where we can go, keeping in mind where we might like to end up. We may end up somewhere else, and maybe that's even better than what we thought of. But the way will be step by step.

All of us now are in new territory. Of course, we also are in old territory for part of it, but our growth exists in new territory, step by step. A turn to the right—"That looks like it fits"—or to the left, or straight ahead, or pausing until something changes—whatever that might be. New direction, new experience: going toward something is always present In the now, but what steps you take and how you allow yourself to check, "Does this fit for me?" is your experience. Others cannot tell you your experience. If you find a path that someone else used, and it fits for you, use it. However, if it doesn't fit, it is of no value to you, even though it may have been traveled by many people before. Make your path as you go, knowing that at the other end there is light and an outcome.

Begin to set your sights on how you can support yourself in further growth. Remember that you always take your resources with you: your ability to see and hear and touch and taste and smell, to feel and to think, to move and to speak, and to choose. Those are always with you. And their conditions are in terms of how clear and loving you are to yourself, how free you are to comment.

At this moment, visualize or think of the world as being full of opportunities and full of challenges. It has a variety of possibilities in it: joy, love, excitement, pain, anger, frustration. These are all expressions of humanness. They all contain energy, and they all can be used in your service if you know how to do it. So you need not block any of them or try to hide any of them. Instead, find the energy that you can use for yourself within each expression.

As you move further, you can become aware that that which is part of you, which you try to hide, does not die. It works in the dark, as though pinching from underneath. So you need to give yourself permission to let it all out, to acknowledge it all, knowing that as the shepherd you can use what you need at a moment in time, and you have much.

At this time, I'd like you again to remind yourself of your self-esteem maintenance kit: of how you are related to all the energies of the world, the center of the earth, the heavens, and the people outside of you. And let yourself know again, through your breathing, through your message of love to yourself, that you create in yourself that being which can become healthy, peaceful, creative, exciting.

So once again, you leave your sanctuary, board your magic carpet, and bring yourself fully here, feeling relaxed, as though you were waking from a long sleep. And when you are ready, open your beautiful eyes.

Our Bodies Respond to Our Thoughts

So now, being in touch with your breathing, see if you can feel it flowing to all parts of yourself. And then again be aware of the five stages of change: status quo; introduction of a foreign element, which means something new; chaos, the displacement experience that happens, which is itself the opportunity for something new; the gradual sorting out of what new can happen; and then the practice of the new before a new status quo appears. This is the story of life as we keep on going through these stages, which are now high in our awareness and experience.

And again let yourself come in touch with your resources. As you do, see that sacred place where you and your resources live, and notice your ability to see and hear and touch and taste and smell, to feel and to think, to move and to speak; and know all of these parts are what help you and guide you to new possibilities. Look at that which you have, and use it wisely and well if it fits. And notice that which you yet do not have, which you want to acquire, and know that because you have resources you can acquire anything you want.

Perhaps at this moment we can become aware that age is never a factor in our development. What is, is our consciousness and our connectedness with ourselves. Our bodies respond to our thoughts about ourselves, and so adding another year gives us new opportunities to practice the sorting. And it's in the sorting that our vitality remains and grows. To let go of that which no longer fits, to honor that which we have, and to add that which we yet do not have is the process of life. This is what gives us vitality.

Are we farther along at this point in becoming aware that we are always able to contact the energy from the center of the earth and from the heavens? That ability to contact is a factor of awareness and not of anybody's whimsy. Nor is it a factor of our behavior. The earth, with its ability to ground us, and the heavens, to give us inspiration, are always there. They do not go away. They are ready to receive us when we open ourselves to their wonderful energies.

And let's remember at this point our self-esteem maintenance kit, perhaps becoming more aware as we practice using our detective hat first; as we practice our integrity with the real yeses and nos that we need to say and to know they are about fit and not about who's valuable; and as we take our courage stick and move ahead, dragging our fear behind, knowing that as we step into our courage, fear begins to diminish. And to know we always have with us our golden key, which enables us to ask about anything, to look at anything. And then we have our wisdom box, which is actually our connector to the wisdom of the universe. It too is always there, and the reason we don't hear it sometimes is because it has been separated from us by our own fears, worries, and rules—which we can now let go.

Perhaps it becomes more clear that as we take charge of us, we then are able to move from the inside to the outside, to people outside of us who are ready to greet us, meet with us, connect with us. And also to know that even if they are not ready, we can shine our light in their direction and move on. Maybe next time their readiness will be there.

We have spent this time in meditation, and I ask you now just to be aware of any ways you might see differently, any changes you might notice. Perhaps at this time you might find on your path that there are more things you would like than you ever dreamed of before. You may find that you want some forms of something which do not appear to be in those forms at this moment, but in another form. What I'm doing is asking you just to become aware of that wonderful self of yours as it has taken in things that might help you to move farther toward your own evolvement.

And now I wonder if you would allow yourself to send energy to any persons, yourself included, who need your energy, who may at this moment need support. And let us send that energy now.

Find the Balance Within

As we begin, I wonder if you would be willing to give yourself a message that you will find the time at the beginning of your day to enter into a meditation. What we really do in meditation is to affirm the fact that we are divine beings, that we are capable of learning, that we are loved and lovable, that we are manifestations of life, and that we are shepherds of our own lives—reminding ourselves of what we have.

If you were to do this in the confines of your own home, in your own room, in your own private space, it might take only a few minutes. You might even put on music for yourself to help you along. There are so many things that happen in the outer world that can take us away from our feelings of value, from our ability to relax. Perhaps in the interest of self-care you might give yourself permission to meditate, so that after a while it becomes automatic, that meditation is as important as washing your face.

Now, as you are seated, check to see how your body is related to the chair you are sitting on, how your feet are related to the floor, and whether you are in balance, with no one part carrying more than another part—like that wonderful telescope I once touched in Lake Geneva, Wisconsin, that weighs some forty tons but could be moved by a slight pressure of my forefinger.

Weight is never the problem. Balance is the goal. Just check to see if all the parts of yourself are carrying their weight, and check if your body is in such a place so that your circulation can move easily. Check your body for any tight places, because tightness will impede the circulation of your blood and your breath. Look around inside your body. Listen for any responses from your body, like a little ache here, a little dryness there, a little murmur from some other place. Acknowledge the messages from them, and then let the tension go out on an outgoing breath.

And maybe we can know, more than at any time before, that any messages from our body, which might include pain, are the way we hear the cry and the need. Our pain could be a good friend, to let us know that something is out of balance. When we are out of balance, we have a way to know about it.

So now, as you give yourself permission and pay attention to your being related to your chair in a fashion that your body and you feel good about, let yourself again become aware, in a deeper way, of the relaxation of your body.

Recognize again that your breath can do what it needs to do when your body is relaxed. As you are in touch with your feelings of relaxation and the sensation of taking a breath in, be aware that this adds up to new strength—a new way to give yourself new power, through relaxing your body and taking in your breath consciously. So the next time you feel a sense of panic or some related form of fear, remember—relax, breathe. And remember what it means: that adding new strength enables you to be more centered and to use your resources more accurately. So you will then see better, hear better, move better, think better, and act better—better, meaning more appropriately.

You could almost make a formula for yourself: "When I'm relaxed, when I'm breathing in awareness, I increase my strength and I make it possible for me to cope more precisely, appropriately, and creatively with what is outside of me. Perhaps I can even count on and know more fully that the event is not the problem. It will be my coping with it that determines what happens. My coping depends on my relaxation, my breathing, and my strength. Added to all of this is love of myself."

And so at this moment again move inside and give yourself a message of love for you in whatever form that means, "I value me, I love me." Knowing that as we increase awareness and love for ourselves, we increase our ability to love and deal effectively, fairly, and lovingly with other people.

Much is at stake, then, for us to love ourselves. Yet for many of us, loving ourselves was not something that was part of our growing up. It was expected of us to love others; but that didn't

106

work well, because we didn't know how to love ourselves. Now maybe that can change. So again be in touch with your breathing and a message of value for yourself. And perhaps you can also be aware that as you strengthen your love for yourself, you strengthen your courage to take the risks you need to take, to change the behavior you engage in—behavior, meaning only your actions.

Also become aware of your ability to know more about your actions, and to know even more that maybe your actions do not represent your intent.

And now I wonder if you would be willing to do a little inventory of yourself. Just see if on a conscious level you are aware of new ways you have successfully directed yourself in your behavior, ways that now get you closer to your goals. For instance, you can ask for what you want now, knowing you have a better chance of getting it and also knowing that what you want at this moment may not be forthcoming, but that it is a question of fit, rather than of your value. As you are reviewing new actions you can take on your own behalf, it results in a closer relationship between you and your behavior. None of your past can interfere with you, because you have your resources. And while you are in touch, can you also be aware of the resources that you have to help you reach your goals?

Looking into your self-esteem maintenance kit, become adept at using it: your detective hat to look before you judge; your medallion, your symbol of integrity, to say the yeses that you feel are accurate and the nos as well, and to know they relate to fit and not to worth; your courage stick, to take ahead of your fear; your golden key, to allow you to ask the unaskable; and the wisdom box that connects you with all intelligence on the planet, so never again will you need to feel ignorant or limited. You carry all your growth potential with you.

Using Your Self-Esteem Maintenance Kit

Going to that place where you give yourself that message of appreciation for you, is it beginning to feel more and more as a way of loving yourself and making yourself strong? And at the same time, is your ability increasing to have loving, clear, strong, real relationships with others? Are you learning in the face of someone else's criticism that criticism is a manifestation of little self-worth asking for recognition? By your attention you may give their self-worth recognition, and the criticism doesn't matter.

Now, can you remind yourself of your playground where you can go—playing, creating, adding, having a wonderful time? Giving yourself permission, move there at any point you wish.

Perhaps you can become aware that the newer learning techniques are all based on having an image: an image within enhances the opportunity to achieve your goal.

Give yourself permission to move to the sanctuary where *The Book of Me* is kept and see what you have written. What happened to you? In this book you don't have to write it all down, you just have to experience it. And it is there when you want to come and look at it again. Is there anything that you experienced that you'd like to share later? Some new possibility, some new awareness, new struggle, new bubble, or something new about something old?

Now putting the book back on the shelf and moving outward, back here, let yourself remember your maintenance kit: your detective hat, your medallion, your wishing stick, your wisdom box, and your golden key.

And now, move deep inside to the place where you keep your resources: those things that you always have with you, which you'll take to any unknown place, because that will be your security: your ability to see and hear, to touch and taste and smell, to feel and think, to move and speak, and to choose. To choose out of all of that which fits you well at this moment, and to notice that which you no longer need and let it go with your blessing—it helped you at some point. Give yourself permission to add what you need at this moment that you yet do not have. And know that you can get it because of your resources.

And also because you are a creature in this universe—a being—you are connected with the energy from the center of the earth—always, not just now and again, but always, and this gives you your ability to be grounded. You have only to become aware. The energy doesn't stop. And you are connected with the energy from the heavens, which brings you your ability to make life have color and feeling and juice, pictures and sensing—a very essential quality.

Recognize that these two wonderful resources play as partners to each other. They are not in opposition. For years and years and years, these two were opposed. Men could only have the cognitive or the groundedness; women could only have the intuitive or the inspirational. Men had no intuition and women had no feet. Or men had no heart and women had no head. That doesn't fit any-more. We all have both. In our current evolvement, wholeness means that each has both.

As we allow ourselves to continue our evolvement, we feel ourselves expanding, getting richer in our abilities, getting wiser and also more confident as living beings, as achievers—whatever we want. And as we combine our energies into this process, they provide us with joy as we move our creative parts into action.

And now at this moment, give yourself permission to become aware of what is developing between you and other people— indeed, perhaps between you and the many people in the world you have not yet met . . . the feeling of connectedness.

Now let your awareness go to your self-esteem maintenance kit. And perhaps give yourself even more energy and support. Really become acquainted with this kit, and let it be there for you at any time you need it. Perhaps already you've seen the value of discovering with your detective hat before judging with your black robes. Perhaps you've also been aware that it becomes easier to say the yeses you really feel and the nos you really, really feel.

Perhaps the sound of your wisdom box is stronger and feels closer to you. You're getting more acquainted with what it contains—a link between you and the universe. All the intelligence and awarenesses that have ever been can move to you through that box. And in your own special storage place of senses, you can get more and more acquainted, until finally you know that your cognition and intuition are like a hand in a glove. They fit together and do not fight each other. A glove does not become a hand, a hand does not become a glove. Each in itself is an entity all of its own. And so it is with your cognitive and affective self.

You need to ask yourself how many times you've already used your courage stick in the face of fear to lead you where you wanted to go . . . perhaps finding out that as you move with your courage, your fear diminishes, and your wonderful golden key allows you to open anything. You enter and, depending on your wisdom box, your courage stick, your medallion, and your discovery or detective hat, you decide whether you go farther or not. That kit is always with you, you really can't lose it. It's like your self-esteem: you only need to be connected with it.

Standing Centered in the Ebb and Flow of Life

Now, I'd like you to board your magic carpet and move to that place where you keep and have your sacred sanctuary. As you move on this magic carpet or whatever vehicle you wish to use to get to your sanctuary—your sacred sanctuary—you may feel an excitement moving to this place you've been to before. It's only yours, and no one else comes, but that's because you want it that way. It's our privacy: that part deep within us that perhaps we don't want to share or share at this time.

And as you move toward that place, you take out your golden key and open the beautiful door so effortlesly. Moving inside, you see the windows, the light, the fixtures, the furniture, the carpets, the floors. And everything is as you would like it, just exactly the way you would like it. Then you move again to that place that's already familiar: that place on the bookshelf where you see that book that says *The Book of Me,* and your name is under that. It's a beautiful book bound in wonderful leather, printed perhaps in gold or silver—whatever you like. You take your book off the shelf.

It's been a while since you've visited this place that is here in your meditation, but turn to the page that is of this date. It will be blank at the moment. And I would like you to write, in your mind (and of course it will go in the book), a paragraph that summarizes what you learned yesterday, that you want to put down. Write down what you learned, and if you don't want to write, draw a picture.

And as you are drawing or writing, you are becoming aware that any change you've made will require other changes. Perhaps you're becoming aware of that. What happens when you give up the idea that "I'm no good," for instance? What happens when you begin to become aware that you are a manifestation of life? That "I am of value"? What else changes for you?

This will be wonderful in the book! You can no longer indulge yourself with old ideas of "I am sick, bad, dirty" once you learn to love yourself. Rather, you can now try on the new clothes and attitudes of someone who values oneself, takes pride in looking in the mirror, enjoys things, enjoys talking about oneself, and enjoys loving oneself. And as you're writing or drawing in your book, perhaps you can be aware that each change, each new learning, opens up a whole network of possibilities.

And while you have this wonderful book in your hands—*The Book of Me*—I'd like you to thumb through backwards and let the book fall open at a place of some past experience in your life—a pleasant experience for you, maybe when you were two or five or ten or twenty. And then let it fall again to a new place, and here you may see a challenge that made you feel bad or momentarily took you off your center. Let yourself be in touch with that. And now let it fall to another place; and in this place where you see so clearly, let yourself know in relation to what is happening, either happy or sad, that you are standing centered and are related to the ebb and flow of life—the ups and downs and ins and outs. None of these ups and downs and ins and outs are things that define you, but rather are things that give you opportunities for new copings.

And now be ready to leave this place. I would like you to give yourself permission that whenever you feel like it, for the rest of your life, you'll allow yourself to go to this place if it fits for you— this private, wonderful place where you can think about, paint, draw, and write about your life and you in your book of learning, *The Book of Me.* This interlude could be a basis of how you approach the rest of your life.

And so you put the book on the shelf and leave your wonderful sanctuary. Locking the door and boarding your magic carpet, you come back here, being aware that all the time, there or here, you are in contact with the energy from the center of the earth, from the heavens, and with others outside of you. That is your birthright. And perhaps you can be more aware than ever before that whatever it was you learned in your past and which does not serve you well now, you can let go in the interest of learning something that serves you better.

And as we come to the end of the meditation, I would like to suggest that you have a means of clearly putting out your wishes. I'd like to suggest that you use a colored balloon to put your wish in, and let it go out to the universe, knowing that the universe is friendly to you and is waiting to hear your messages. It will act on all messages having to do with growth for you. The air is full of balloons with messages inside that have to do with your growth.

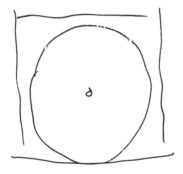

About the Authors

Virginia Satir (1916-88) was internationally recognized for her creativity in the practice of family therapy. Based on a deep conviction that people are capable of continued growth, change, and new understanding, her life work was to improve relationships and communication within the family unit.

She is often called the Columbus of family therapy, having initiated many of the present practices in that field and beyond. Satir wrote *The New Peoplemaking* and *Conjoint Family Therapy*, and coauthored many more, including *Satir Step by Step, The Satir Approach to Communication, Say It Straight,* and *The Satir Model*.

For more than twenty years, she reached out to the people of numerous countries. She taught professionals and the public how to be more fully human, how to be whole and congruent, and how to enjoy a deeper sense of peace. Four months prior to her death, for example, she spent one month in the Soviet Union teaching her skills.

During the last five years or more of her life, Virginia's openness to her own spirituality and life force not only enriched her meditations but influenced her teachings, her relationships, and her own sense of being.

Anne Banmen spent considerable time with Virginia Satir during a three-month training schedule in Manitoba in 1972. From 1981 until Satir's death in 1988, Anne spearheaded and managed most of Satir's two-day workshops in the Northwest. She also attended more of Virginia's training events in Canada and the United States.

After raising three sons and working many years as a registered nurse, Anne retired in 1988 to spend her time writing. She completed her first novel, *Dreams on Hold,* after editing this book, and is currently working on her second novel and an anthology of poems. She and her husband, John Banmen, are also working on a book that shows how Satir applied her change process in large groups.

 **John Banmen** first met Virginia Satir in early 1970, and then, from 1980 to 1988, he spent between six and seven weeks annually with her. Their relationship provided him with many in-depth learning and teaching experiences.

John has been active in numerous associations and organizations, such as the Avanta Network (on the Governing Council and Directorate of Training), the Canadian Guidance and Counselling Association (as president), the British Columbia Association for Marriage and Family Therapy (as president), and the American Association for Marriage and Family Therapy (as a board member).

He has taught at the University of Manitoba and the University of British Columbia and has worked for the Manitoba government as a former Deputy Minister of Corrections and Rehabilitation Services. He has led Satir Model workshops in Venezuela, China, Hong Kong, Canada, and the United States. He has been on staff at the Satir International Summer Institute since 1981.

He is presently a psychologist and family therapist in private practice, as well as the Coordinator of Child and Family Services, Delta Mental Health Centre, British Columbia Ministry of Health.